NICHIREN

NICHIREN:

THE BUDDHIST PROPHET

MASAHARU ANESAKI

GYAN

Published by

GYAN

Gyan Publishing House
5, Ansari Road
Daryaganj, New Delhi-110002
Phone: 011-47034999, 9811692060
E-mail: books@gyanbooks.com

Distribution Network
gyanbooks.com
India, USA, Canada, UK, Australia

ISBN: 978-93-7014-315-9 (PB)

First Published, 1916

2nd Impression 2025

Printed at: Gyan Press, Delhi.

NICHIREN
Author: MASAHARU ANESAKI

NICHIREN

THE BUDDHIST PROPHET

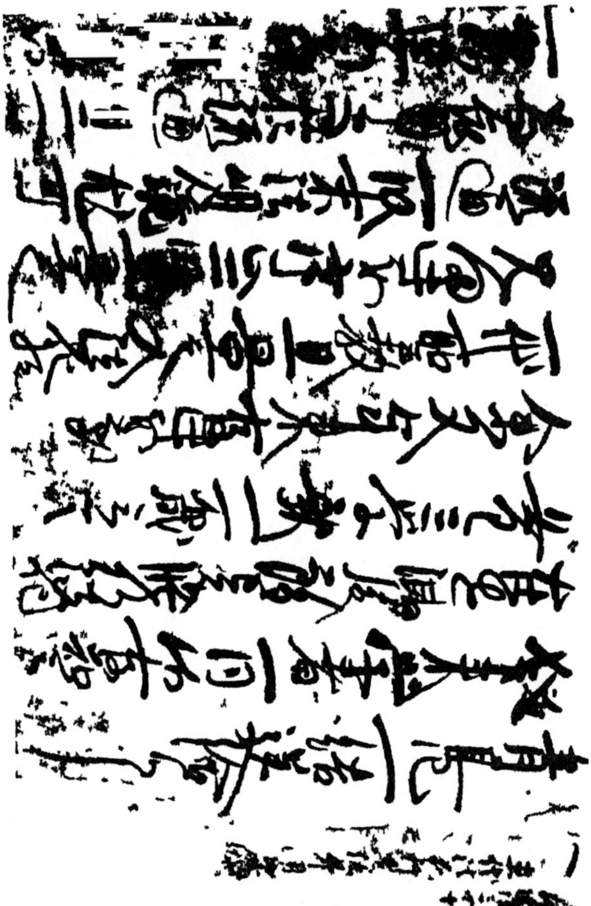

REPRODUCTION OF AN AUTOGRAPH MANUSCRIPT
BY NICHIREN

NICHIREN
THE BUDDHIST PROPHET

BY

MASAHARU ANESAKI, M.A., Litt.D.

PROFESSOR OF THE SCIENCE OF RELIGION
AT THE IMPERIAL UNIVERSITY OF TŌKIŌ AND
PROFESSOR OF JAPANESE LITERATURE AND LIFE AT
HARVARD UNIVERSITY, 1913–15

CAMBRIDGE
HARVARD UNIVERSITY PRESS
LONDON GEOFFREY CUMBERLEGE
Oxford University Press

PREFACE

SINCE the appearance of Professor James' " Varieties of Religious Experience," the attention of scholars has been strongly drawn toward men of original religious experience, with emphasis on the psychological point of view, disregarding doctrinal considerations. A conspicuous result of the change brought about by this book is that religious psychology has been extended from a study of material taken from the average masses, to the study of strong personalities and their characteristic faith. The primary motive of the present work is to contribute to this newer branch of religious psychology a study of a man who has been comparatively unknown to Western scholars. Another impetus to thepublication of this study was derived from the encouragement given by Professor Royce. After reading his book, " The Problem of Christianity," I presented to him an essay on the Buddhist conception of life, as a counterpart of his chapter on the Christian doctrine of life. A reference to Nichiren made in that paper led me to tell the senior philosopher of Harvard more about the Buddhist prophet. The present volume is a result of his advice and encouragement to write something on Nichiren.

Nichiren's personality has various peculiar interests of its own. Besides the points which I have tried to bring out in this book, it is deserving of special mention that a great amount of material for the study of his life is available in his numerous writings, amounting to more than four hundred essays and epistles. Not only have most of them been proved to be authentic, but about one-third are preserved in Nichiren's original hand-writing, while many others have come down to us in old manuscripts made by his disciples or later followers. These authentic writings contain ample and trustworthy sources for the study of his life and thought, and nearly every step of his development, his struggles, and his faith can be clearly traced in them; for Nichiren was a man who told much about himself, his experiences and ambitions, his thoughts and sentiments. Moreover, he was an unexcelled calligrapher, and his autographs have a characteristic vividness of expression, due to the picture-like forms of the Chinese ideographs. Thus, not only can his thoughts and the incidents of his life be learned from his own words and sentences, but the modulations and changes of sentiment and emotion can be closely followed in his writings. It is rare that the works of an ancient author are so well preserved and furnish us so abundantly with the means of investigating his career and ideas as in this case.[1] In the present sketch all traditions and legends of later growth have been excluded, and all the main points, as well as many minor details, are related exclusively on the basis of Nichiren's own statements. For this reason it may be regarded as virtually a record of Nichiren's own confessions, and as such, it will, I hope, be found a useful study in the religious psychology of a prophetic leader.

To the intrinsic interest of the life of Nichiren as a Buddhist reformer of the thirteenth century, may be added the fact that there has been a noteworthy revival of his teaching and spirit in modern Japan. Details about this revival, as well as the growth of Nichiren's influence after his death,

[1] Omitting remarks on editions of his writings, I note here that these writings are cited in this book from Rev. B. Katō's edition, of 1904, and that the majority of the autographs are now accessible in splendid photographic reproductions.

will be treated in my forthcoming book on the Religious and Moral Development of the Japanese. Perhaps I may be permitted to say a little concerning my personal relation to the Nichirenite revival. It was during my stay in England and India that my dear friend, Chogyū Takayama, was converted to Nichiren's faith and that I criticized him in correspondence. Takayama's conversion caused a great stir, and though there were adverse critics, there were also enthusiastic admirers, especially among the younger generation, who flocked to the ardent convert and his accepted prophet. Since then, many societies have been organized for the study — both historical and religious — of Nichiren, and their membership comprises students and scholars, lawyers and business men, military and naval officers. When I returned to Japan in June, 1903, my friend had already been dead six months; but his influence was rapidly growing, and he who had once been called "the Nietzsche of Japan" was regarded as the standard-bearer of the Nichirenite revival. The task of editing Takayama's writings gave me occasion to study the process of his conversion, together with the life and personality of his prophet. Further studies have brought me into closer and closer touch with Nichiren's faith and thoughts. The consequence is that in writing this book I have always been tempted to tell the story fully, and have found it difficult to decide how much should be omitted. At any rate, I offer this little volume to the public with a full confidence that I have not misrepresented the great teacher.

I cannot let this book appear without expressing my deep gratitude to Professor Josiah Royce and Professor George F. Moore. The former, as I have said above, showed his interest in the subject and gave me valuable aid by reading through the manuscript and suggesting various points that might with advantage be recast, for all of which I am very grateful. Professor Moore has kindly revised the manuscript, made arrangements for publication, and consented to read the proofs. Indeed, without such encouragement and assistance from my fatherly colleagues at Harvard this publication would not have been possible. The present volume will always recall to me pleasant memories of my delightful stay at Harvard, during my two years of work there. I hope that I may soon give another humble sign of my homage to Harvard by a publication dealing with the religious and moral history of Japan, which was the subject of my lectures there.

M. ANESAKI.

CAMBRIDGE, MASSACHUSETTS,
June 9th, 1915,
the six hundred and thirty-fourth anniversary of the arrival of the Mongol armada at the Bay of Hakata.

CONTENTS

CHAPTER I

Nichiren and His Time

CHAPTER II

Nichiren's Birth, Studies, and Conversion. The Lotus of Truth

CHAPTER III

Nichiren's Public Appearance and Persecution

CHAPTER IV

An Interlude and a Narrow Escape

CHAPTER V

The Threatening Mongol Invasion and the Sentence of Death

CHAPTER VI

The Exile in Sado and the Ripening of Nichiren's Faith in His Mission

CHAPTER VII

The Climax of Nichiren's Life; the Graphic Representation of the Supreme Being

CHAPTER VIII

Release and Retirement; Further Confirmation of His Faith

CHAPTER IX

A Paradise on Earth and the Holy See

CHAPTER X

Silent Prayer and Anxious Watching

CHAPTER XI

The Last Stage of Nichiren's Life and His Death

APPENDIX

The Buddhist Conception of Reality

NICHIREN

THE BUDDHIST PROPHET

NICHIREN, THE BUDDHIST PROPHET

CHAPTER I

NICHIREN AND HIS TIME

IF JAPAN ever produced a prophet or a religious man of prophetic zeal, Nichiren was the man. He stands almost a unique figure in the history of Buddhism, not alone because of his persistence through hardship and persecution, but for his unshaken conviction that he himself was the messenger of Buddha, and his confidence in the future of his religion and country. Not only one of the most learned men of his time, but most earnest in his prophetic aspirations, he was a strong man, of combative temperament, an eloquent speaker, a powerful writer, and a man of tender heart. He was born in 1222, the son of a fisherman, and died in 1282, a saint and prophet.

His time was a most significant epoch in the history of Japan, in political and social, religious and moral aspects. New energies were at work on every side, and new inspirations were the need of the time. Nichiren passed his life of sixty years in combating the prejudices of the age and in giving warnings to the authorities and the people, not only in religious matters but in state affairs. His personality was partly a product of his time, but he lived both in the past and in the future, being convinced of his predestined message and aspiring for future realization of his ideals.

Nearly seven hundred years had passed since the introduction of Buddhism into Japan. It had become the religion of the state, and its hierarchies had attained the power and dignity of state authorities, but inner decay was manifesting itself, and the corruption of the clergy was becoming appalling. The central government, firmly established since the seventh century, was disintegrating through the degeneration of the court bureaucracy. The actual power was transferred to the hands of the military clans. The passing of the luxury and grandeur, "Peace and Ease," of the court nobles in Miyako, and the establishment of the military dictatorship at Kamakura, far away in an eastern province, impressed the people immensely. The cherry blossoms, in full bloom, were suddenly scattered by a frosty storm. Not only did the poets so feel and sing, but the people were aware of the great changes going on around them.

In addition to these changes, the minds of the Buddhist leaders were in turmoil, excited by the prophecy of a great crisis to occur about that time — a crisis not only for Japan, but for the whole world. An old Buddhist tradition distinguished three periods of the Buddhist religion (*Dharma*, or Law) after the death of its founder. The first thousand years made up the age of the Perfect Law, in which the monastic discipline was strictly observed and the believers were sincerely pious. The second millennium, the age of the Copied Law, was a time during which faith and morality declined, but piety was shown in the foundation of numerous temples and sanctuaries. The third age, the ten thousand years after that, was to be the age of the Latter Law, a reign of vice and strife. Though there were minor variations in the tradition as regards the time divisions, all Japanese Buddhists believed in the apocalyptic legend as a whole.

And since they put Buddha's death in 949 B.C., they believed that the last of the three ages began in the year 1052 A.D., twenty-four years after the death of the Regent Michinaga, with whom the pomp and splendor of the court life in Miyako reached its culmination.

What form of Buddhism would be best suited to the coming days of degeneration was a question which had occupied the thought of many Buddhist leaders since the ninth century. Saichō, who founded a new centre of Buddhism on Mount Hiei, near the then new capital Miyako, in the beginning of the ninth century, meant the foundation to be a preparation for the approaching days of the third age. He said: "Approaching is the end of the age of the Copied Law, and nigh is coming that of the Latter Law; the ripe time for the propagation of the unique truth expounded in the Lotus of Truth."[1] Thenceforward, none of the leaders escaped the influence of the prophecy, and serious thought on the Latter Days was growing during the eleventh and twelfth centuries. And it was Nichiren who came to the front as the most ardent follower of Saichō, and was destined to encounter perils on that account.

When Nichiren appeared in public with his cry of warning, two hundred years had passed since the supposed beginning of the Latter Days. The vicissitudes of the rising and falling clans, culminating in the establishment of the military dictatorship by the Minamotos, seemed to manifest the dangerous signs of the times. The irremediable corruption of the hierarchies gave clamorous testimony to the decline of the religion. Let us consider the political and religious con-

[1] Or, The Lotus of the Perfect Truth, Saddharma-pundarīka in Sanskrit, the most important scripture of Japanese Buddhism, of which we shall learn more later on.

ditions against which Nichiren stood forth as a warning prophet.

Early in the thirteenth century, the power of the ruling clan Minamoto passed gradually into the hands of their usurping major-domos, the Hōjō family. The latter ruled with the modest title of *Shikken*, or Commissioners, with the puppet dictatorship ostensibly over them. Their government was famous for strict execution of justice and for simplicity of administration; and the Commissioners themselves set examples of simple life and stern justice. But their modesty was, in the eyes of those who regarded them as usurpers, merely a means to their ambition — the ambition to secure popularity — and their equity but a method of solidifying their rule. Indeed, the Hōjōs understood how to sacrifice everything *in titulo* to the power *de facto*, and to become the real rulers of the nation by pushing aside the Imperial family and the titulary Dictator. A firm peace was established, and economic conditions prospered; but there was something lacking in it. There prevailed a feeling among the thoughtful minority that the "country of the gods"[1] was not being actually ruled by its legitimate rulers, the descendants of the Sun-goddess.

Availing themselves of this unexpressed dissatisfaction, the Imperial party framed a plot against the Hōjōs in 1221, a few months before the birth of Nichiren. The plot was defeated, and the Commissioner government dared to banish prominent members of the Imperial family to remote islands, and to put an infant on the throne. Thus, the Hōjō power was consolidated and immensely increased, although these rulers still retained the modest title of Commissioner. The

[1] This appellation of Japan came into vogue after the latter half of the twelfth century, and was closely connected with the belief that the Imperial family were descendants of the Sun-goddess, the chief national deity.

resentment of the discontented patriots only grew deeper in consequence of the forcible suppression of the movement, but politically their cause had already been hopelessly lost. It was under these circumstances that Nichiren appeared on the public platform as a spokesman of the patriotic cause whose utterances were deeply tinged with religious fervor. He declared that the nation would be ruined, unless the fundamental principle of the national life should be restored, that is, unless the people were governed by rulers legitimate both in title and authority. Herein lay the national standpoint of his religious ethics, and this plea attracted to his teaching many warriors who were imperialists in principle or covert malcontents against the existing régime. This was also the reason why the Hōjō government, as we shall presently see, treated the clamorous protestant as a traitor.

Turning to another matter, the religious conditions, Nichiren saw similar evils, closely connected with the political and social disorders. The far-reaching plan of Dengyō, the reformer of the ninth century, for establishing the centre of Japanese Buddhism on Mount Hiei and unifying its church organization, had been partly realized. But even this partial attainment of the ideal of a state church was of merely temporary duration, because the relations established between the church hierarchy and the government bureaucracy had had a corrupting influence on both of them. The centralization of government and the consequent accumulation of wealth in the capital were concomitant with the development of ecclesiastical power and the growth of secular aims and motives among the clergy. The government fell into the hands of the Fujiwara oligarchy, who now became the supporters of the church with its rituals and mysteries; and the priesthood degenerated into tools of the ambitious aristocrats, by promising them the supernatural aid of religion, and by supplying them with elaborate ceremonies for the gratification of their over-refined tastes. The final result was the collapse of the effeminate court nobility and the rise of the military class. To the eyes of those — few in number — who adhered to the ideal of Dengyō, the political disintegration seemed to be a necessary consequence of the ecclesiastical degeneration. Nichiren was one of these, and the one who was most severe in attacking the existing régime — both political and ecclesiastical.

The chief cause of the degeneration of the Buddhist Church lay, as Nichiren thought, in its promiscuous adoption of Shingon mysticism, a form of Buddhism contaminated with Hinduism and other alien elements. It was this admixture that appealed to the court nobles and supplied them with brilliant spectacles and occult mysteries. It was this secularization, or vulgarization, of religion that had obscured the high ideals of Dengyō and reduced his institutions on Hiei to instruments of greed and vice. Even after the fall of the Fujiwara nobles, the supporters of Hiei, this religion of occult rites exercised its influence far and wide among the people at large through the superstitious practice of magic and sorcery. Therefore, Nichiren's bitterest attacks were directed against this corrupt religion and its centre, Hiei. He firmly believed that the sole way to restore Dengyō's religion consisted in adhering faithfully and exclusively to the scripture, the Lotus of Truth.

Another form of Buddhism, in which Nichiren saw a curse, was the worship of the Buddha Amita. This was a special development of Buddhist faith which emphasized the simple-hearted devotion to Amita, the Buddha of Infinite Light and Life, the Lord of the Western Paradise. This worship seemed to Nichiren to be a desertion of the Buddha Śākya-muni, the genuine founder of Buddhism and the Lord of the Universe, as he was revealed in the Lotus of Truth. The gospel of salvation by the all-redeeming grace of Amita Buddha had crept into the institutions of Hiei, and, later, produced an independent sect, through the personal inspiration of the pietist Hōnen and by its appeal to distressed hearts in the turbulent times toward the end of the twelfth century. Amita Buddha was, in the eyes of Nichiren, nothing but a usurper of the true dignity of Buddha, and the piety of multitudes toward the supposed savior but a manifestation of the hysterical tendency of the age. Nichiren boldly declared that those who believed in this usurper were destined to fall to the nethermost hell, while the Shingon mysticism was denounced by him as a religion that was ruining the vitality of the nation.

Nichiren's third object of attack was a school of Buddhist monastic discipline. In the twelfth century a reaction against the corruption of the hierarchy took, with certain reforming leaders, the shape of enforcing a strict observance of the monastic rules. They systematized the principles of Buddhist ethics from the standpoint of monastic discipline. This school was called *Ritsu*, or Disciplinary School, and developed a one-sided rigorism, which manifested in the course of time the evils of formalism. Training in morality, under rules, cultivated a tendency to practise virtue merely for the sake of individual salvation. Self-satisfaction easily grew into self-conceit, which often tempted the adept in these extraordinary ways of life to make his attainments the means of attracting popular admiration and reverence.

Moreover, the slavish and formal observance of disciplinary rules which had originally been intended for Hindu monks, aroused antagonism in those who adhered to Japanese ideas and customs. Nichiren, as a nationalist and an advocate of a broader Buddhism, could not fail to protest vigorously against the *Ritsu* Buddhists. He called them traitors to their country.

The introduction of a new Buddhist school, called *Zen*, or the Meditative School, increased the religious confusion. Zen was a simple method of training intuitive insight by the practice of meditation, which aimed at revealing the primordial purity of the cosmic soul in each individual soul. Riddle-like questions were given by the master which the disciples had to solve, sitting in meditation, by avoiding the usual process of reasoning and trying to discover an unexpected light by a flash of illumination. This new method of mental training and spiritual drill commended itself to the minds of military men, and they found in it a very beneficial exercise for keeping their composure and preparing for resolute action. Not only did Zen reject systematic thought on religion and ethics, but it induced those robust but rude men to take pride in self-assertion and often to run to an excess of individualism. Nichiren saw in this new method of Buddhist meditation a rebellion against the genuine Buddhism of the Lotus, as well as a fruitful source of rampant selfishness. "Devil" was the name given by Nichiren to the Zenist, and the "devils" were threatening the national integrity of Japan and the authority of the true Buddhism.

Shingon occultism ruining the nation, Ritsu methodism betraying the country to foreign customs, Amita-Buddhism leading people to the hells, and Zen meditation alluring men to devilish pride — these four were declared by Nichiren to be the greatest curses of the age. The violent antagonism of Nichiren was due to his exclusive faith in the teachings of the scripture, Lotus, as representing the genuine and deepest truth of Buddhism. Now, we shall see why and how he arrived at this conviction, and what the Lotus of Truth is.

CHAPTER II

NICHIREN'S BIRTH, STUDIES, AND CONVERSION

The Lotus of Truth

NICHIREN was born on the seacoast of the south-eastern corner of Japan, in a fishing village surrounded on the north by undulating hills and washed by the dark blue waves of the Pacific Ocean on the south. Tidal waves have washed away the part of the seacoast where his father's house stood, and today the spot is pointed out in the depths of the wonderfully clear water, on the rocky bottom of the sea, where lotus flowers are said to have bloomed miraculously at the birth of the wonderful boy. His father was a fisherman, and doubtless the boy was often taken out in the father's boat, and must have enjoyed the clear sky and pure air of the open sea. When in later years, during his retirement in the mountains, a follower sent him a bunch of seaweed to eat, the old hermit wept as he called to mind his early memories of the seaweeds, which are, indeed, a charming sight as they are seen through the transparent water. Far away from the effeminating air of the Imperial capital, far away from the turmoils and agitations of the Dictator's residence, the boy grew up in the fresh and invigorating atmosphere of a seaside village, in the midst of unadorned nature — wooded hills and green trees, blue waters and sandy beaches. The inspiration of nature and the effect of association with the simple, sturdy people are manifest in each step of Nicheren's later career, in his thoughts and his deeds. The new light was to come out of the East for the salvation of the Latter Days — this prophetic zeal of Nichiren is in large measure to be attributed to his idea about his birth, and to the surroundings of his early life.

In 1233, when the boy was eleven years old, his parents sent him to a monastery on the hill known as Kiyozumi, the "Clear Luminosity," near his home. The reason is not given, but it was in no way an exceptional or extraordinary step; in those days many a father did the same, whether from motives of piety or for the sake of the boy's future career. The peaceful and innocent days of the boy novice passed; he was made an ordained monk when he was fifteen years old, and the religious name given by his master was Renchō, or "Lotus-Eternal." Doubts grew with learning, because too many tenets and practices were included in the Buddhist religion of his days, and the keen-sighted youth was never satisfied with the incongruous mixture in the religion he was taught. "My wish had always been," he tells us in his later writings,[1] "to sow the seeds for the attainment of Buddhahood, and to escape the fetters of births and deaths. For this purpose I once practised, according to the custom of most fellow-Buddhists, the method of repeating the name of Amita Buddha, putting faith in his redeeming power. But, since doubt had begun to arise in my mind as to the truth of that belief, I committed myself to a vow that I would study all the branches of Buddhism known in Japan and learn fully what their diverse teachings were." His distress of mind was, however, not over a merely intellectual problem, but was a deeply religious crisis; and, indeed, the young monk was then passing through so violent a struggle of religious conversion that he at last fell into a swoon, following a fit of spitting blood. It is said

[1] *Nichiren's Works* (ed. Katō, Tokyo, 1904), p. 1770.

that during this swoon he saw, in vision, Kokuzō, the deity of wisdom.

This happened when Renchō was seventeen years old, and in the next year we find him studying under a teacher of Amita-Buddhism in Kamakura, the residence of the Commissioners. The uneasiness of the young monk was not allayed, and his quest of truth was not satisfied by the teachers who were accessible in the provinces. Renchō then went to Hiei, the greatest centre of Buddhist learning and discipline, where he stayed from 1243 to 1253, pursuing a varied course of study and training. During these years he also visited other centres of Buddhism, where special branches of Buddhism were taught and practised, and extended his study even to Shinto and Confucianism. The results of all this study and investigation are shown, not only in the erudition of his later writings, but in the comprehensive breadth of his doctrine. But the range of his studies never diverted him from his central problem: What is the true form and the unique truth of Buddhism? On the contrary, as he progressed in knowledge, the conviction gradually grew strong in his mind that the truth is *one*, and that the essence of the Buddhist religion — nay, of human life — is not manifold. "I had gone to many centres of the religion," he says in reminiscence, "during those twenty years, in the quest of Buddhist truths. The final conclusion I arrived at was that the truth of Buddhism must be one in essence. Many people lose themselves in the labyrinth of learning and studies, through thinking that every one of the diverse branches might help to the attainment of Buddhist ideals."[1] Wherein, then, did the young zealot find the unique truth?

[1] *Works*, pp. 1770–71.

Fierce internal struggles, wide study, and prolonged thought brought this sincere seeker after truth to the final conviction that the scripture, " The Lotus of Truth," was the deposit of the unique truth, the book in which the Lord Buddha had revealed his real entity, and on which the great master Dengyō had based his religion and institutions. The name Renchō was now exchanged for Nichiren, which means Sun-Lotus; the Sun, the source of universal illumination, and the Lotus, the symbol of purity and perfection, were his ideals. Nichiren's firm belief was that the Lotus of Truth was not only the perfect culmination of Buddhist truth, but the sole key to the salvation of all beings in the latter days of degeneration. Thus, all other branches of Buddhism, which deviated from the principle of the exclusive adoration of this scripture, were denounced as untrue to Buddha, as we have already seen in Nichiren's condemnation of the prevalent forms of Buddhism. Nichiren's idea was the restoration of Buddhism to its original purity, and to the principles propounded by Dengyō; but what he understood by restoration was quite different from our modern idea of historical criticism. The truths are eternal, but the method should be a simple one, available for all, especially for men of the Latter Days, and without regard to differences among them in wisdom and virtue. These convictions of Nichiren had a complicated background of philosophical thought, in accord with the general trend of Buddhist speculation, and as a result of his learning. But all these doctrines and arguments were fused by the white-heat of his faith and zeal; that is, he simplified the whole practice of religion to an easy method, that of uttering the " Sacred Title " of the Scripture.

The Sacred Title meant the exclusive adoration of the truths revealed in the book, Lotus, practised in the repetition of the formula: "*Namu Myōhō-renge-kyō,*" that is, "Adoration be to the Scripture of the Lotus of the Perfect Truth!" This formula is, according to Nichiren, neither merely the title of the book, nor a mere symbol, but an adequate embodiment of the whole truth revealed in that unique book, when the formula is uttered with a full belief in the truths therein revealed, and with a sincere faith in Buddha as the lord of the world. Nichiren's thought on this point will be more fully expounded further on, but here let us see just what he meant by the Lotus of Truth. He wrote later, in 1275, explaining his position, as follows:

> All the letters of this Scripture are indeed the living embodiments of the august Buddhas, who manifested themselves in the state of supreme enlightenment. It is our physical eyes that see in the book merely letters. To talk in analogy, the *pretas* (hungry ghosts) see fire even in the water of the Gangā, while mankind sees water, and the celestial beings see ambrosia. This is simply due to the difference of their respective karmas, though the water is one and the same. The blind do not perceive anything in the letters of the Scripture; the physical eyes of man see the letters; those who are content with self-annihilation see therein emptiness; whereas the saint (Bodhisattva) realizes therein inexhaustible truths, and the enlightened (Buddhas) perceive in each of the letters a golden body of the Lord Śākya-muni. This is told in the holy text in the teaching that those who recite the Scripture are in possession of the Buddha's body. Nevertheless, prejudiced men thus degrade the holy and sublime truth.[1]

What, then, is taught in this book which Nichiren esteemed so highly, and what led Nichiren to his conviction? The Lotus of the Perfect Truth, or *Myōhō-renge-kyō* in Sinico-Japanese, is an equivalent of the extant Sanskrit text, *Saddharma-puṇḍarīka-sūtra.*[2] The book circulated in

[1] *Works*, p. 1165; cp. ibid., 1126, 1184, 1313, 1317, 1533, etc.

[2] The Saddharma-puṇḍarīka-sūtra, edited by H. Kern and B. Nanjio, St. Petersburg, 1912. An English translation by Kern is in Vol. XXI of the Sacred Books of the East; the French translation of E. Burnouf is entitled, Le Lotus de la Bonne Loi. Beside Kumārajīva's version (Nanjio's Catalogue,

China and Japan in a Chinese translation produced by Kumārajīva in 407. The translation was so excellent in the beauty and dignity of its style that it supplanted all other translations, and was regarded as a classical writing in Chinese, even apart from its religious import. It was on the basis of this book that Chi-ki, the Chinese philosopher-monk of the sixth century, created a system of Buddhist philosophy of religion.[1] This system was called the Tendai school, from the name of the hill where Chi-ki lived; and it was this system of religious philosophy and philosophical religion that was transplanted by Dengyō to Japan as the corner-stone of his grand ecclesiastical institutions.

Nichiren discovered, during his stay on Hiei, that Dengyō's far-reaching scheme of unifying Japanese Buddhism in his institutions on Hiei had been totally obscured and corrupted by the men of Hiei itself, who had imported degenerate elements of other systems. This thought induced Nichiren to make a zealous attempt at restoring Dengyō's genuine Buddhism, and therefore the orthodox Tendai system. This could be done only by concentrating thought

no. 134), there are two Chinese translations; and one of them produced by Dharmarakṣa (Nanjio's Catalogue, no. 138), is much nearer to the extant Sanskrit text than the former. Now as to the rendering of the title, Dharmaraksa has for *sad* the word meaning "true" or "right," like Kern's rendering "true," while Kumārajīva's rendering *myō* is understood to mean "perfect," "mysterious," "subtle." Here the rendering the "Lotus of the Perfect Truth" is according to Nichiren's exegesis.

Moreover, Nichiren, after comparing the two Chinese versions, decidedly preferred Kumārajīva's. The reasons given are several, exegetic and doctrinal; but here it suffices to say that we reproduce passages of the book from Kumārajīva's translation, and as interpreted by Nichiren. For our object is to show how Nichiren derived inspiration from the book through Kumārajiva's version, and chiefly according to the Tendai exegesis. References are made to a Japanese translation by Yamakawa, and for the sake of comparison the Sanskrit text and Kern's translation are referred to.

[1] See Appendix, on the Buddhist Conception of Reality, Part II.

and devotion upon the sole key of Buddhist truths, as promulgated by the two great masters — that is, upon the Lotus of Truth, especially in Kumārajīva's version.

The book, Lotus, was acknowledged by nearly all Buddhists to be sermons delivered by Buddha in the last stage of his ministry, and, as such, called forth the highest tributes from most Buddhists of all ages. Critical study of Buddhist literature will doubtless throw more light on the formation and date of the compilation; but even apart from minute analysis, we can safely characterize the book as occupying the place taken in Christian literature by the Johannine writings, including the Gospel, the Apocalypse, and the Epistles. The chief aim of the Lotus, both according to the old commentators and to modern criticism, consists in revealing the true and eternal entity of Buddhahood in the person of the Lord Śākya, who appeared among mankind for their salvation. In other words, the main object is to exalt the historic manifestation of Buddha and identify his person with the cosmic Truth (*Dharma*), the universal foundation of all existences.

This main thesis of the book is illustrated, supported, and exalted in manifold ways, and there are many side-issues and episodes. Similes and parables, visions and prophecies, warnings and assurances, doctrinal analysis and moral injunctions — all these ramify from the central strand or are woven into it. The whole composition is a symphony in which the chief motive is the identifying of Buddha and Dharma, but the melodies, the instruments, the movements, and even the key-notes vary from part to part; and, naturally, the inspirations imparted by the book varied from time to time, in accordance with the temperaments, the needs and aims, of different ages and persons. Thus, in describing the outlines of the sermons and narratives contained in this wonderful religious book, let us pay attention to the different phases which were emphasized by different teachers, and especially to the points which inspired Nichiren in the several stages of his life.

The book opens with a prelude played in the serene light of the stage, the Vulture Peak idealized,[1] which is illumined by the rays emitted from Buddha's forehead. He sits immersed in deep contemplation, and yet in the air made brilliant by his spiritual radiance are seen not only innumerable Buddhas and saints, who move in the luminous air, but existences of all kinds, down to those in the nethermost purgatories. Heavenly flowers pour upon the place, the quaking of the earth heralds the approach of an extraordinary occasion, and the congregation is deeply moved with amazement and admiration — men and gods, saints and ascetics, demons and serpent-kings — all are tense with wondering expectation of what the Lord Buddha is going to reveal. (Chapter I, Introduction.)

Buddha arises out of contemplation, and what he reveals is that the real import of the *Dharma* is beyond the ordinary comprehension or reasoning, and that only those who put faith in the unique truth promulgated by all Buddhas are enabled to grasp it. What he now means to disclose is the truth of the Sole Road (*Ekayāna*) which has enabled the Buddhas of the past to attain Buddahood, and which is destined to lead all beings, the future Buddhas, to the same attainment. The Truth is one and the goal the same; but the means and methods are not, because the beings to be enlightened are various in character, capability, and inclination. Thus, all Buddhas have entered upon their training and work for the purpose of leading all beings to the same

[1] Cp. Anesaki, *Buddhist Art*, pp. 15–17, and plates II and VI.

height of attainment they themselves have reached, and Śākya-muni is one of these. Yet, mindful of the varying dispositions of the beings to be instructed, Buddha has opened three gateways, one for those who are keen for knowledge and illumination in philosophical truths, that is, for the *Śrāvakas*; the second for those who are inclined to meditation and self-seclusion — the *Pratyeka-buddhas*; and the third for those who wish to perfect themselves along with others — the *Bodhisattvas*. Although these three ways are different in method and in result, they are destined finally to converge to one and the same Sole Road of Buddhahood. The opening of the different gateways is due to the "tactfulness" (*upāya-kauśalya*) of Buddha's educative method, while the basis of all lies in the same Truth, and the aim is universal enlightenment. This idea of tactfulness, or pedagogic method,[1] gave to many Buddhist thinkers a clue to explain the diversity existing within Buddhism, and we shall later see how Nichiren made use of this explanation. (Chapter II.)

The discourse now proceeds to further elucidation of the relation between the final aim and the educative methods. Three parables are adduced for this purpose: the parable of rescuing children out of a burning house; the parable of bringing a prodigal son to the consciousness of his original dignity and properties; and the simile of the rain-water nourishing all kinds of plants (chapters III–V). Śākya-muni, our master, is at the same time the father of all beings, who tries and does everything to save his errant children. The truth he teaches is the universal truth which can finally be realized by all beings in various existences, just as rain-water, one in essence and taste, enables all sorts of plants to grow and flourish, each according to its capacity

[1] "Accommodation."

and disposition. Thus, the tactful achievement of Buddha's revelation is possible, because he has himself realized the truth of existence, and his person is the embodiment of universal *Dharma*.

What is set forth is the aim of all Buddhas, and the efficacy of the truth they reveal to lead all beings to enlightenment. The leader in this work is found in the person of Śākya-muni, and naturally all of his disciples are assured of the highest attainment and made representatives of the future Buddhas. This assurance, called *vyākaraṇa*, is a prophetic revelation given to those earnest Buddhists who would engage themselves to practise the moral perfection of the Bodhisattva. The Bodhisattva is a Buddhist who has expressed his desire to perfect himself by saving others, and taken the vow (*pranidhāna*) in presence of a Buddha, as his master and witness, and who lives his life, dedicating all his goods to the spiritual welfare of all fellow-beings. When a Bodhisattva takes the vow, and his zeal proves worthy of his determined vow, the Buddha, his witness, assures the Bodhisattva of his future attainment, and reveals his destiny by prophesying how and when the final end of Buddhahood will be attained. The vow (Jap. *seigwan*, Skt. *praṇidhāna*), the dedication (Jap. *ekō*, Skt. *pariṇāmaṇā*), and the assurance (Jap. *juki*, Skt. *vyākaraṇa*), make up the three cardinal points in Buddhist ethics for the achievement of the Bodhisattva ideals.

In accordance with this principle of Buddhist ethics, the discourse of the Lotus proceeds (in chapters VI–IX), to reveal the *vyākaraṇa* given by Śākya-muni to his disciples, assuring them their future destiny, as well as telling the remote causes accumulated for its fulfilment. The *vyākaraṇas* given in these chapters are indeed prophecies, but Buddhist thought has never been satisfied without referring future accomplishments to their past causes. This is the reason why chapter VII tells how the start was made by Śākya-muni, in a remote past, when he was a prince and took the vows of Bodhisattvaship before the Buddha Abhijñājñānābhibhū,[1] and how, ever since, the connection between himself and his disciples has been maintained. Just as the vows taken by that prince, have been accomplished and his master's *vyākaraṇa* fulfilled, so will the destiny of his present disciples surely be attained. And thus the prophetic assurance is extended to all Buddhists of the future. These discourses have been a great inspiration to many earnest Buddhists, who have journeyed on the way to their perfection with confidence in the assurance given in these chapters.

The purpose of Buddha's work has been laid down, the assurance given to his followers, and the foundation of the Sole Road explained. The further revelation naturally turns to how the destiny is to be worked out by the Bodhisattvas. The essence of Bodhisattvaship in this sense consists in the adoration paid to the sacred text of the Lotus, the embodiment of universal truths — adoration not only in worship through ceremonies and recitations, but in practising its precepts and preaching its truths to others; in short, in living the life of Truth according to the sermons of the Lotus. The Bodhisattva is the messenger of the Tathāgata[2] (Buddha), the one sent by him, who does the work of the Tathāgata, who puts absolute faith in Buddha and his Truth, and lives the life of Truth, especially by

[1] The name means "the Conqueror of Powers and Wisdom."

[2] *Tathāgata* (Jap. *Nyorai*) means the "Truth-winner" and, at the same time "Truth-revealer." Cp. Anesaki, *Buddhist Art*, pp. 3–5, and 8; also the article "Tathāgata" to appear in Hasting's *Encyclopaedia of Religion and Ethics*.

working to propagate the truths of the Lotus among the degenerate people of the Latter Days. Thus, chapter X, entitled the "Preacher," consists of the injunctions given to the Bodhisattvas to live worthy of their high aim and in obedience to Buddha's message and commission.

A vision follows the injunction, a miraculous revelation, as well as an apocalyptic assurance (chapter XI, entitled "The Apparition of the Heavenly Shrine"). A vast shrine (*stupa*) adorned with the seven kinds of jewels appears in front of Śākya-muni as he is preaching; heavenly hosts surround it, waving banners, burning incense, playing music; the air becomes luminous, iridescent, fragrant; the sky resounds with heavenly music and chanted hymns. Suddenly, the scene is totally transformed, as we see in apocalyptic literature generally. A voice is heard from within the shrine in the praise of Śākya-muni's work and sermons. In the midst of the celestial glories and the hosts of heavenly beings, the Heavenly Shrine is opened, and therein is seen seated the Buddha Prabhūta-ratna,[1] who long since passed away from his earthly manifestation, and has now appeared, to adore Śākya-muni who is still working in the world. The dramatic situation reaches its climax when the old Buddha invites the present one, and the two sit side by side in the Shrine. The joint proclamation made by them is to prepare the disciples for the approaching end of Śākya-muni's earthly ministry, and to encourage and stimulate them to the work to be done after the master's passing away. "Revere the Truth revealed in this holy book, and preach it to others! Any one who will fulfil this task, so difficult to do, is entitled to attain the Way of Buddha, beyond comparison. He is the child of Buddha,

[1] The name means "Accumulated Treasure"; Japanese *Tahō*.

the eyes of the world, and will be praised by all Buddhas." (Chapter XI.) [1]

The admonition is further encouraged by the prophetic *vyākaraṇa* given to Devadatta, the wicked cousin of Buddha, who, because of his long connection with Sākya-muni, will, in spite of his wickedness, attain Buddhahood at a certain future time. Moreover, the assurance of the final perfection is vividly impressed by the instantaneous transformation of a Nāga (Serpent-tribe) girl, who now appears as a preacher of the Perfect Truth and one of the Tathāgata's messengers. The final conversion of the typical wicked man and of the innocent girl indicate that Buddhahood is to be realized by all; and these episodes were always a source of inspiring faith, and encouraged trust in the efficacy of the excellent truth revealed in the book.

After the apocalyptic scene and the miraculous conversion, other practical admonitions are given to the future Buddhas. Two ways of spreading the truth are indicated, one the way of vigorous polemic, the repressive and aggressive method of propaganda, and the other the way of pacific self-training, the gentle, persuasive method (chapters XIII and XIV, entitled respectively the "Exertion," or "Perseverance," and the "Peaceful Training"). The peaceful training in meditation and watchfulness over self was a source of great inspiration to many Buddhists; but greater, at least so far as Nichiren is concerned, was the power inspired by the admonition to perseverance. Indeed, the

[1] Yamakawa, p. 364; Text, p. 256; SBE., pp. 242–243, verses 38–41. The Chinese version makes a separate chapter out of the portion corresponding to Text, pp. 256–266 (SBE., pp. 243–254). This chapter, no. xii, is called the Devadatta, and Nichiren was very particular about this division, for various reasons. In this volume we shall keep to Nichiren's division; and consequently the numbers of the several chapters after this are higher by one than the numbers in the extant Sanskrit text.

characteristic feature in Nichiren's ideal consisted in translating into life the exhortations to strenuous effort, in what he called the " reading of the Scripture by the bodily life," which meant actual life, fully in accordance with the truths taught in the book, especially with the exhortations, encouragement, and assurances contained in this chapter on " Perseverance." As we shall see later, in every hardship and peril which Nichiren encountered, he derived consolation from Buddha's reassurance, and stimulating inspiration from the vows uttered by his disciples to sacrifice everything for the sake of the Truth, and to endure perils, sustained by firm belief in the mission of the Tathāgata's messengers.

With these exhortations given to future Buddhas closes the first grand division of the book, which is the revelation of the Sole Road proclaimed by Śākya-muni in the " manifestation " aspect of his personality. With the fifteenth chapter opens the revelation of his true, eternal, primeval [1] personality, together with the apparition of his primeval disciples, the vows they take, and the mission entrusted to them.[2]

This thought on the two aspects of Buddha's personality is a consummate outcome of religious and philosophical speculation on the transient and the everlasting aspects of Buddha's person and work — a matter touched upon before, when we characterized the book, Lotus, as the Johannine literature of Buddhism. And now, in the last

[1] [" Primeval " is used here and in the sequel of beings, attributes, and relations in a transcendent sphere of reality, in distinction from the world of historical manifestation. — *Ed.*]

[2] Arthur Lloyd, in *The Wheat among the Tares* (p. 79) and *The Creed of Half Japan* (p. 289), totally misinterprets the import, accepted by most Japanese Buddhists, of the division of the book into these two parts.

half, is revealed the primeval Buddhahood or the entity and functions of the Buddhist Logos. So long as the Buddhists regard their master as a man who achieved Buddhahood at a certain time, they fail to recognize the true person of Buddha, who in reality from eternity has been Buddha, the lord of the world. So long as the vision of Buddhists is thus limited, they are unaware of their own true being, which is as eternal as Buddha's own primeval nature and attainment. The Truth is eternal, therefore the person who reveals it is also eternal, and the relation between master and disciples is nothing but an original and primeval kinship. This is the fundamental conception, which is further elucidated by showing visions reaching to the eternally past as well as to the everlasting future.

Having been quickened by Buddha's urging, the Bodhisattvas in the congregation ask the Lord to entrust to them the task of propagating and perpetuating the Truth. Quite contrary to their expectation — and ours — they are counselled to keep themselves quiet. While they are astonished at the Lord's dissuasion, he summons the innumerable hosts of saints, who appear out of the earth from all quarters. Among them four figures are conspicuous, who were never known before to any in the assembly, and whose names, they are told, are Viśiṣṭa-cāritra, Ananta-cāritra, etc.[1] The endless hosts, following the four leaders, pay adoration to Buddha, and pledge themselves to work for the perpetuation of the Truth and the salvation of all beings. The surprise of the other members of the assembly is voiced by Maitreya, the highest of the Bodhisattvas, who asks Buddha, "Who are these saints who have appeared out of earth?"

[1] The names mean, "Superior-conduct," "Endless-conduct." The former, *Jōgyō* in Japanese, was the one with whom Nichiren was most eager to identify himself.

The answer is that they have existed from all eternity, and have always been Śākya-muni's disciples — an answer which puzzles the inquirers still more, because their idea of Buddha as a man who no great while ago attained Buddhahood under the Bodhi-tree at Gayā is incompatible with the statement that these miraculous beings existing from eternity are his disciples (chapter xv, entitled the "Issuing-out-of-the-Earth"). How Nichiren believed himself to be a reincarnation of Viśiṣṭa-cāritra, or Jōgyō, will be seen later on; and his reference to an eternal and primeval discipleship to the eternal Buddha can be understood by turning to this scene.

The sixteenth chapter, entitled the "Duration of the Tathāgata's Life," is meant to solve the puzzle, and to reveal the eternal existence of Buddha's personality. The Buddha who was born and is going to die, or to disappear from among mankind, is but a manifestation, and his (apparent) death is in order to dispel the disciples' vain hope of having his earthly manifestation with them forever. Neither is birth the beginning, nor death the end of life; the true life extends far beyond both of these commonly assumed limits. Things come and pass away, but truth abides; men are born and disappear, but life itself is imperishable. Buddhahood is neither a new acquisition nor a quality destined to destruction. The One who embodies the cosmic Truth, Buddha, the Tathāgata, neither is born nor dies, but lives and works from eternity to eternity; his Buddhahood is primeval and his inspiration everlasting. How, then, can it be otherwise with any other beings, if only they realize this truth and live in full consciousness of it? Thus, the revelation of the everlasting life discloses the infinite measure of the Tathāgata's life, which means at the same time the share of the true Buddhists in the eternal life of Buddha, and in the inextinguishable endurance of the Truth.

It was this teaching of the eternal life, both of Buddha and of ourselves, that inspired in Buddhist belief boundless strength, and led Tendai and Dengyō to systematize their theory about the primeval dignity of Buddhahood and the pre-established possibility of our supreme enlightenment. Nichiren inherited and emphasized these doctrines as the very basis of his religious thought, but we shall see later how he applied the conception of the primeval relationship between the Lord and his disciples to the moral life of mankind.

The climax of the revelation is followed by a series of encouraging assurances given by Buddha, and of enthusiastic vows made by the disciples and celestial beings. The revelation of the eternal past is thus followed by the assurance for the everlasting future. The past and the future are united in the oneness of the Truth, by the unity of purpose, methods, and power, in all the Buddhas of all ages — in short, in the Sole Road of Truth. This is the cardinal teaching of the Lotus, as in other Buddhist books or systems; but the special emphasis laid by the Lotus, particularly in the last twelve chapters, is upon the question, Who shall really be the one who will perpetuate and realize this truth of the Sole Road? The Truth abides eternally, but it is an abstraction, a dead law, without the person who perpetuates the life of the Truth. The Buddha Śākya-muni, in his human manifestation, was the one, the Tathāgata *par excellence*; but who shall be the one in the future, nay in the present, in these days of degeneration and vice ? This was the question of Nichiren, who at last, as the result of his hard experience and perilous life, arrived at the conclusion that he himself was the man destined to achieve the task of the Tathāgata's messenger.

All of the remaining chapters (XVII-XXVIII), the "Consummation and Perpetuation" of the truths revealed, have always been a strong inspiration to Buddhist piety. The narratives and prophecies contained in them gave consolation in various ways, and the saints in the stories were the objects of pious devotion on the part of many Buddhists. Especially the compassionate help promised to Buddhists by Avalokiteśvara, the god of mercy (chapter XXV), was regarded as a powerful incentive to grateful piety. Other saints or deities appearing in these chapters were regarded as protectors of Buddhists, and their worship consisted in devotion to them and dependence on their divine grace. In short, for most Buddhists before Nichiren, the admiration of these chapters and the worship of the divine beings who appear in them amounted to praying for benefits, and even to superstition.

Now Nichiren interpreted the "Consummation and Perpetuation" in a totally different manner. The inspiration he derived from these narratives was a spirit of emulation, instead of mere piety; the life of the true Buddhist was to be lived in emulating the courageous and compassionate spirit of the divine beings and the vows they uttered. This was due to Nichiren's peculiar conception of the whole scripture, namely, that it was a book not to be read simply by the eyes, or merely understood by the mind, but to be "read by the body," that is, by flesh and blood. The truths revealed therein were, for Nichiren, the records of the true Buddhist life, which was realized by the saints of the past, and therefore to be striven for by all Buddhists of the coming ages.

Seen in this light, the whole book, and especially the part on the "Consummation and Perpetuation," was a storehouse of exhortations and precepts, prophecies and assurances, given to the future Buddhists, especially to those living in the latter days of the world. For instance, take chapter XXI, on the "Mysterious Power of the Tathāgata." It is not only a revelation of Buddha's own divine work, but an assurance given to all Buddhists, that the "Mysterious Power" should be realized and embodied in every Buddhist's actual life. Nichiren regarded as of the highest importance a passage pointing to a definite person, designating him as "this man."

> Just as the light of the sun and moon
> Expels all dimness and darkness,
> So *this man*, living and working in the world,
> Repels the gloom (of illusion) of all beings.[1]

How this statement was taken as a prophecy concerning the leader of the true Buddhism in those days, that is, Nichiren himself, will be seen as we follow his growing consciousness of his mission. To take another instance, there is a passage in chapter XXIII, on the Bodhisattva Bhaiṣājya-rājā,[2] foretelling the propagation of the Lotus of Truth in the fifth five hundred years after Buddha's death.[3] Herein Nichiren saw another prophetic assurance given to his mission.

Of great importance, in Nichiren's view, was the story of the Bodhisattva Sadāparibhūta, a previous life of Buddha himself, told in the twentieth chapter.[4] The story is this. While Buddha was still striving for Buddhahood, he was a monk, and used to salute every person he met as a future

[1] Yam., pp. 567–568; Text, chapter XX, verse 13, p. 394; SBE., p. 369.
[2] The name means "Medicine-King"; Japanese, *Yaku-wō*.
[3] Yam., p. 596; Text, p. 420, lines 13–14; SBE., p. 391.
[4] Sanskrit text, chapter xix.

Buddha, because he was convinced that every one was destined eventually to be so. The people, however, took this salute as an insult, and in turn insulted and abused the monk. He endured all this, but never changed his way of saluting others, or his conviction that every one was a Buddha-to-be. Therefore he was called the "Constantly-revering."[1] This story is told as an occurrence in the past, and also as an example for all Buddhists, especially for those living among the evil-disposed men of degenerate ages. It was this aspect of the story, indicating an underlying bond connecting the true Buddhist of the past with his successor in any age, that inspired Nichiren and kept him ever perseverent throughout all persecutions. Thus, in *his* mind this story of the "Constantly-revering" saint was nothing else than another version of his own life, which was also foretold in the vows of endurance as recorded in the thirteenth chapter. The same spirit of endurance for the sake of the Truth, and the same life in emulation and practice of the ardent vows of the ancient saints — this was what he found in the story, and derived from it incentive and consolation.

The Lotus of Truth is a rich treasury of religious inspiration and moral precepts, prophetic visions and poetic imagery, philosophical speculations and practical admonitions. From this book, all ages, and every man in Buddhist countries, derived some sort of instruction and inspiration, each according to his needs and disposition. Most Buddhists of a speculative trend of mind occupied themselves in elaborating the teaching of the oneness of

[1] The Sanskrit name Sadā-paribhūta, certainly means the "Constantly-abused," but Kumārajīva rendered the name by the "Constantly-revering," that is, *Sadā-aparibhūta*, or with a different termination indicating the present participle. Japanese, *Jō-kufyō*.

Truth, the doctrine of the Sole Road, notwithstanding the three gateways opened by Buddha in chapter II, on "Tactfulness." Many others, inclined to fantastic imagination, and delighted with supernatural glories, were keen for heavenly visions and apocalyptic scenes. Many others, again, found objects of worship in the deities of mercy and benefaction, such as Avalokiteśvara. Much was written on the Lotus — philosophical treatises, miracle stories, poems, and prayers; the book also inspired many painters and sculptors, and we have a rich store of works of art whose subjects are taken from it.[1] But there was none, until Nichiren "read" the book in his original way, who derived from it such a wonderful power of strenuous, militant life, and thereby lived a life of striving toward the ardent zeal exemplified by primeval disciples of Buddha. Indeed, Nichiren deemed himself to be an embodiment of the Scripture, a personal version of its teachings and prophecies and a living testimony to them.

How did he carry out his life in accord with this idea and attain to a full conviction of his mission, foreordained in the Lotus of the Perfect Truth?

[1] See Anesaki, *Buddhist Art*, Chapter I.

CHAPTER III

NICHIREN'S PUBLIC APPEARANCE AND PERSECUTION

THE young monk, now no longer a seeker after truth, but a reformer filled with ardent zeal, bade farewell to the great centre of Buddhism on Hiei and went back to the old monastery on Kiyozumi, which he had left fifteen years before. He visited his parents, and they were his first converts. His old master and fellow-monks welcomed him, but to their minds Nichiren, the former Renchō, was nothing more than a promising young man who had seen the world and studied at Hiei. Keeping silence about all his plans and ambitions, Nichiren retired for a while to a forest near the monastery. Every one in the monastery supposed that he was practising the usual method of self-purification which they themselves employed; but, in fact, Nichiren was engaged in a quite different task, and occupied with his original idea, neither shared nor guessed by any one else.

The seven days of his seclusion, as the tradition says, was a period of fervent prayer, in preparation for launching his plan of reformation and proclaiming his new gospel. When his season of meditative prayer had reached the stage when he was ready to transform it into action, Nichiren one night left the forest and climbed the summit of the hill which commands an unobstructed view of the vast expanse of the Pacific Ocean. When the eastern horizon began to glow with the approaching daybreak, he stood motionless looking toward the East, and as the golden disc of the sun began to break through the haze over the vast expanse of waters, a loud voice, a resounding cry, broke from his lips. It was "*Namu Myōhō-renge-kyō*," "Adoration be to the Lotus of the Perfect Truth!" This was Nichiren's proclamation of his gospel to heaven and earth, making the all-illumining sun his witness. It happened early in the morning of the twenty-eighth day of the fourth lunar month (May 17) 1253.

The proclamation of the Lotus of Truth, with the sun as witness, was, indeed, the first step in translating into action the ideal symbolized in his name, the Sun-Lotus. After this unique proclamation, Nichiren came back among human beings, and at noon of the same day, in an assembly hall facing south, he preached his new doctrine, and denounced the prevailing forms of Buddhism, to an audience composed of his old master and fellow-monks, and many others. There was none who was not offended by his bold proclamation and fierce attack. Murmurs grew to cries of protest; and when the sermon had been finished, every one assumed that the poor megalomaniac was mad. The feudal chief ruling that part of the country was so incensed that he would not be satisfied with anything short of the death of the preposterous monk. This lord, who was Nichiren's mortal foe throughout the subsequent years of his mission, was watching to attack Nichiren, who was now driven out of his old monastery. His master, the abbot, pitied his former pupil, and gave instruction to two elder disciples to take Nichiren to a hidden trail for escape. It was in the dusk of evening that Nichiren made his escape in this way. The sun, which at its rising had beheld Nichiren's proclamation, the sun which at noon had witnessed Nichiren's sermon, set as the hunted prophet made his way through the darkness of a wooded trail; only the evening glow was in the sky. What must his thoughts have been? What prospect could he have cherished in his mind for his future career and for the destiny of his gospel?

The expelled prophet now went on missionary journeys in the neighboring provinces, and finally settled down in Kamakura, the seat of the Dictatorial government. While he was studying further the religious and social conditions of the time, and looking for an opportunity to appear again in public, the city of Kamakura was the scene of many frightful events. There were rumors of plots against the Hōjōs, and family strife arose among them; in addition to these things, storms, inundations, earthquakes, famines, comets, followed one another in swift succession. The people were panic-stricken, and the government could only resort to the offerings at Shinto sanctuaries and to the Buddhist rites of the Shingon mysteries. Nichiren himself describes the conditions as follows: [1]

> We have seen many signs in heaven and in earth; a famine, a plague—the whole country is filled with misery! Horses and cows are dying on the road-sides, and so are men; and there is no one to bury them. One half of the population is stricken, and there is no house that has entirely escaped.
>
> Hence many minds are turning to religion. Others, again, in accordance with the doctrines of the Secret Shingon, use copious sprinkling of holy water from the five vases. . . . Some write the names of the seven gods of luck on pieces of paper, and affix them by the hundreds to the door-posts of their houses, whilst others do the same with the pictures of the five Great Powerful and the various (Shinto) gods of Heaven and Earth. . . . But let men do what they will, the famine and the plague still rage; there are beggars on every hand, and the unburied corpses line the roads.

[1] The quotation is taken from the opening of Nichiren's essay, "*Risshō Ankoku Ron*," of which more will be said later. The English is from the pen of Arthur Lloyd, *The Creed of Half Japan*, pp. 307–309. The language of the original is more rhetorical, in accordance with the style of the time; in later years Nichiren wrote with less flowery rhetoric.

Out of pity, not only for the people stricken by these calamities, but on account of the superstitious practices in which they took refuge, Nichiren pondered in his mind the question, What are the causes of these evils, and how can they be averted?

In attacking the problem, Nichiren's thought naturally turned to the unique authority of the Lotus, in contrast to the syncretistic practices of the prevailing Buddhism. Yet he was not satisfied until he had made a further investigation of the sacred books and found various prophecies concerning calamities which should befall the people who degraded the true Buddhist religion by resorting to superstitions. He retired, for this investigation, to a monastery furnished with a good library. There he wrote and rewrote his ideas, which finally took shape in an essay entitled "*Risshō Ankoku Ron*," which means "The Establishment of Righteousness and the Security of the Country." [1]

In this essay Nichiren fearlessly pointed out the degeneracy of the people and the foolishness of the rulers. The heaviest responsibility for the miseries of the time he ascribed to Amita-Buddhism,[2] by which both the government and the people were led astray from righteousness. Moreover, he gave a prophetic warning to the nation that, if it did not turn at once to the unique Truth, the country would experience more disastrous calamities, especially a

[1] The first version was finished in 1259, and the final one in 1260. The latter is shorter, and in the form of a dialogue. See Lloyd, chapter xxv, from which the following quotations are made.

[2] In this essay, the most vehement attack was directed against Amita-Buddhism and its propounder Hōnen; while in Nichiren's other writings from the same period attack was also directed against Zen. Later on, the two other branches, Shingon and Ritsu, were similarly criticized — definitely, first in the letters sent to the authorities in 1268. Hence the adverse criticism against these four branches of Buddhism became an integral part of the Nichirenite dogmatics.

foreign invasion [1] and a rebellion. His vehement expression runs as follows:

> Of all the misfortunes . . . , but one remains that we have not yet experienced, the misfortune of foreign invasion. . . . When I consider these Scriptural prophecies and then look at the world around me, I am bound to confess that both the gods and the minds of the people are confused. You see the fulfilment of the prophecy in the past; dare we say that the remaining prophecies will fail of their fulfilment ?

This warning was followed by an admonition to the nation to be converted to Nichiren's religion, based on the sermon of the Lotus. The vehement prophet would not be satisfied unless all other forms of Buddhism were suppressed and their leaders severely punished. Thus he concludes:

> Woe unto them! They have missed the entrance into the gate that leads to the true Buddhism, and have fallen into the prison-house of the false teachings. They are fettered, entangled, bewildered. Whither will their blind wanderings lead them ?
>
> Ye men of little faith, turn your minds and trust yourselves at once to the unique Truth of the Righteous Way! Then ye shall see that the three realms of existence are (in reality) the Kingdom of Buddha, which is in no way subject to decay; and that the worlds in the ten directions are all Lands of Treasures, which are never to be destroyed. The Kingdom is changeless, and the Lands eternal. Then how shall your bodies be otherwise than secure and your minds serene in enlightenment ? [2]

Not only were these words preached to the masses on the streets and in the parks, but the written document was presented to the government authorities (in the seventh month of 1260). The government was shocked, the ecclesiastical dignitaries were enraged, and instigation from behind the scenes stirred up a mob which attacked Nichiren's hermitage

[1] This prediction was based on statements in several Buddhist books, and its realization in the following years immensely strengthened Nichiren's faith.

[2] The idea of the earthly paradise will be seen later. The English version is partly Lloyd's, and partly mine.

and burnt it down. Nichiren escaped the peril through the darkness of the night, and fleeing out of Kamakura, went on a missionary journey in adjacent provinces. There, more converts were made, and among them not a few of the warrior class, the local chiefs who were not under the direct control of the Dictator. The suspicion in which the government held Nichiren increased, and when he came back to Kamakura in the following year, he was officially arrested, and finally sentenced to banishment and sent to the desolate shore of the peninsula Izu (in the fifth month of 1261).

In this place of exile, Nichiren found bare shelter with a fisherman and his wife, in the midst of threatening dangers. How deeply he felt his obligations to these simple and faithful converts is shown in the letters written to them later, wherein they are likened to Nichiren's parents, perhaps in a former life. His hardest trials did not last long. More converts were made, and Nichiren's message found a sincere response in the unprejudiced hearts of the country folk. Yet he was an exile; he had been repeatedly attacked, and had some narrow escapes from death; his future showed no bright prospects, and his hope of converting the nation as a whole seemed to be very remote, if not totally vain. His thought turned to the question whether his mission would be fulfilled, and he re-examined the Scripture with reference to this problem.

Nearly ten years had passed since Nichiren had proclaimed his new gospel, and these years had been full of adventures and dangers. The threats and perils heaped upon him, as well as the disasters which filled the people with terror, seemed to him not mere chance, but the necessary consequence of the conflict between the blindness of the people and the compassionate cure proposed by him. All this—the causes and effects, the present calamities and the future destiny—gave him new assurance that every prophecy in the Scripture would certainly be fulfilled. The thing which most strongly confirmed his faith in the Scripture and his enthusiasm for it was the discovery that every phrase of the vows of perseverance, as set forth in the chapter on "Perseverance," had been, and was being, realized, step by step, in his own life. The ardent spirit of the vows found its closest counterpart and echo in his fiery personality and perilous career.

See what the Scripture tells us! Buddha's disciples, beholding the amazing vision of the Heavenly Shrine, and hearing the encouraging exhortation, take together the vows of fidelity and endurance.

> O Exalted One! be little anxious for us!
> After Thy great decease,
> In the evil ages full of fears and dangers,
> We shall proclaim the supreme Scripture.[1]

This was what Nichiren had done, and he was now suffering for it.

> There will then surely be malignant men,
> And they will deride us and abuse us,
> Lay upon us with weapons and sticks.
> All these things we shall bear with endurance and perseverance.

Does this not mean, Nichiren thought, the laymen, the rulers, and the people, who antagonize the Truth because of their dislike for righteousness? Did they not threaten him with sword and fire? Again:

> In the Latter Days there will be monks,
> Who, being malicious and crooked in mind,
> Will pretend to have attained what is not really attained,
> And their minds will be full of vain pride.

[1] This and following passages, Yam., pp. 389-393; Text, pp. 271-274; SBE., pp. 259-261.

Were not the monks always the instigators of the persecutions? Traitors to Buddha, companions of devils, worshippers of strange deities, men of vain pride — these are Nichiren's bitter enemies. Is not the prophecy being fulfilled by them? Further:

There will be those who dwell in forests (*āraṇyaka*),
Living in tranquillity and wearing the regular robes;
They pretend to practise the true monastic life,
And despise all other men.

They will preach to laymen,
Simply for the sake of fame and profit;
And yet they will be revered by the people,
As if they were endowed with the six supernormal powers. . . .

Are not all abbots and bishops men of this kind? Observe how some of them pretend to be Arahants, and are believed by the people!

In the evil days of the ages full of turbulence
There will be many fears and dangers;
There will be men possessed by devils,
And they will abuse and insult us.

By revering Buddha and putting confidence in him,
And by wearing the armor of forbearance,
We shall endure all these perils,
For the sake of proclaiming this Scripture.

We shall never be fearful in sacrificing our bodily life,
But always regard the true Way as the highest cause;
And thus we shall, throughout all coming days,
Stand for the cause committed to us by Buddha.

O Exalted One! Thou may'st be assured,
Even when the vicious monks of the turbulent ages,
Being ignorant of the sermons preached by Buddha,
According to his tactful method,

Shall revile and rebuke us;
And we be repeatedly driven out of our abodes,
And kept away from our sanctuaries.
Even then, we shall endure all these injuries,
By keeping ourselves to Buddha's decrees.

In whatsoever cities or villages,
There may be any who would seek the Truth,
Thither we shall surely go
And preach the Truth entrusted to us by Thee.

We are Thy messengers, O Exalted One!
We have nothing to fear from any people,
We shall proclaim the Truth, to deserve Thy commission.
Thou may'st be assured and rest secure.

Now we take these vows in Thy presence,
And in the presence of all Buddhas
Who have come from the ten quarters.
May'st Thou, O Buddha, know our intention and determination!

Nichiren saw all this being fulfilled in himself, but had to anticipate yet more persecutions. In later years he referred most earnestly to the passage which tells how the preachers of the true religion should be repeatedly expelled from their dwellings, because it was *his* actual experience. Thus he found all his career foretold in the Scripture, and deemed that he was faithfully observing the vows of perseverance. "The Twenty Stanzas of Perseverance" was his favorite expression, which he was proud to embody in his life.

He formulated these reflections and hopes in an essay, and in its conclusion his convictions are vividly set forth:[1]

It is said in the chapter in the Scripture on Perseverance (chap. XIII) that, in the fifth five hundred years of the religion, there would appear opponents of the Truth, of three kinds. The present time is just in this period of the fifth five centuries, and I see clearly the existence of the three kinds of opponents. . . . It is said in the fourth fascicle of the Scripture:[2] "Even in the life-time of the Tathāgata, there are manifold animosities shown toward this Scripture; how much more will it be so after his passing away?" Again, in the fifth fascicle:[3] "All over the world, the people find it so difficult to believe that they

[1] *Works*, p. 429.
[2] Yam., p. 327; Text, p. 230, lines 7–10, SBE., p. 219.
[3] Yam., p. 418, chapter xiv; Text, p. 290, line 12; SBE., p. 275.

antagonize (the Truth)." Further on:[1] "We shall not care for bodily life, but do our best for the sake of the incomparable Way"; and similarly, in the sixth fascicle: "We shall sacrifice even our life." . . From what we see in these passages it is evident that we are not entitled to be propagators of the Lotus of Truth, unless we call forth the hatred of the three kinds of opponents. One who does so is the propagator of the Truth, and yet he is destined to lose life on this account.

We can here see clearly how Nichiren was prepared for any perils, and how ready to encounter even greater dangers, leaving his fate to the destiny of the true Buddhist as prophesied in the Scripture. To him dangers and persecutions were the very signs of his being the genuine believer of the Truth.

As a man trained in the analytic method of Buddhist philosophy, Nichiren proceeded to determine the position he occupied in the perpetuation of the religion, after the model of his great master Tendai,[2] deriving his material from the five conditions, or "principles", of his mission. First, as to the doctrine, his gospel was based exclusively on the scripture, Lotus, which was the perfect consummation of Buddhist doctrines, before which the teachings of all other branches of Buddhism must lose weight and authority. Second, as to the capacity of the people taught, mankind in the degenerate age of the Latter Days could be trained only by the simplest expression of truth, not by a complicated system of doctrine, nor by an intricate process of meditation and mysteries. Third, as to the time, his time was the age of

[1] Yam., p. 392, chapter xiii; Text, p. 273, verse 15; SBE., p. 260.

[2] *Works*, pp. 424–429, dated the tenth of the second month (March 1) 1262. The essay is entitled "*Kyō-ki-ji-koku shō*," or "Treatise on the Doctrine, the Capacity, the Time, and the Country." Cp. the fivefold knowledge (*pancaññū*) of Buddha, concerning instruction, in *Anguttara*, v. 131: the principle, the truth, the degree, the time, and the congregation.

the Latter Law, in which the scripture, Lotus, alone would remain available for the salvation of all. Fourth, as to the country of its promulgation, Japan was the land where the true Buddhism would prevail, and whence it should be propagated throughout the whole world. Lastly, as to the order of the successive rise and fall of systems, all other forms of Buddhism had severally done their work, and Nichiren's time was ripe for the acceptance of the Lotus, as the sole authority in religion. All the five conditions for the supremacy of the Lotus seemed to Nichiren to be fulfilled, and he regarded himself as the man destined to accomplish the work of realizing the prophecies contained in the Scripture.

This was his conviction and consolation; yet it is noteworthy that the personal thesis is not so clearly and vividly stated in this essay, as it is in his later writings. Let us cite his own words. After having explained the five conditions, he says:

> One who would propagate the Buddhist truth, by having convinced himself of the five principles, is entitled to become the leader of the Japanese nation. One who knows that the Lotus of Truth is the king of all scriptures, knows the truth of the religion. . . . If there were no one who "read" the Lotus of Truth, there could be no leader of the nation; without a leader, the nation could do naught but be bewildered, . . . and fall to the nethermost hells in consequence of degrading the Truth.[1]

After these remarks, he enumerates the passages concerning the difficulties to be encountered by the promulgators of the Truth, meaning to apply the passages to himself. It was these convictions that consoled Nichiren in the midst of dangers, and inspired him with a firm belief in the future of his mission. But his conviction regarding his destiny, as

[1] *Works*, p. 427.

well as his remote connection with the sages of the past, remained to be more exactly defined in writings from his second exile. In the essay before us, we see a decided progress in Nichiren's trust in the Lotus of Truth, which had started on a doctrinal basis, and was destined to bring him to more personal conviction of his prophetic mission.

CHAPTER IV

AN INTERLUDE AND A NARROW ESCAPE

IT was in the second month (April) of 1263, that Nichiren was released from his banishment in Izu. The reason for the release is unknown, but his return was a triumph for Nichiren. By the rising of the mob, and during his exile, his abode had been devastated, his disciples ill-treated, and some of his lay followers threatened with confiscation of their properties. Yet they remained faithful to the prophet and his instructions; and when the master came back to Kamakura, they flocked to him, and welcomed him with tears of joy. It seems that some of them wished to see their master mitigate his trenchant attacks upon other Buddhists, believing that the true religion could be propagated without antagonizing others. This is reflected in Nichiren's strong insistence, in an essay written immediately after his return,[1] on the proposition that an exclusive devotion to the unique truth of the Lotus is the necessary condition to salvation. It was impossible for him to modify his attitude, for he was a man who had passed through perils and was thereby strengthened in the conviction of his own mission and destiny. He now preached in a manner more intransigent than before, and drew a strong contrast and a sharp line of demarcation between his gospel and Amita-Buddhism as well as Shingon mysticism. The forcible arguments and

[1] The essay entitled "*Ji-Hokke Mondō-shō*", or "A Catechism on the Method of Holding the Lotus of Truth", written in 1263. *Works*, pp. 465-476. Further reference to this writing is made below.

vehement invectives, directed especially against these two schools, exhibit the method of Nichiren's proselyting, which he now stated explicitly and systematically.

Irreconcilably pugnacious toward his opponents, yet tenderly persuasive toward his followers, Nichiren almost always combined these two sides of his propaganda; but the writings produced within a few years after the first exile show, decidedly more than the earlier ones, a wonderful combination of the two. The delicate sentiment shown in his tender persuasions is now remarkably united with admonitions to honest faith and pure heart. The essay referred to above, written in the form of a catechism, is an example of this. After affirming the necessity of an exclusive devotion to the Lotus, it proceeds to emphasize the efficacy of simple-hearted faith: [1]

> If you desire to attain Buddhahood immediately, lay down the banner of pride, cast away the club of resentment, and trust yourselves to the unique Truth. Fame and profit are nothing more than vanity of this life; pride and obstinacy are simply fetters to the coming life. . . . When you fall into an abyss and some one has lowered a rope to pull you out, should you hesitate to grasp the rope because you doubt the power of the helper? Has not Buddha declared, "I alone am the protector and savior"? [2] There is the power! Is it not taught that faith is the only entrance (to salvation)? There is the rope! One who hesitates to seize it, and will not utter the Sacred Truth, will never be able to climb the precipice of Bodhi (Enlightenment). . . . Our hearts ache and our sleeves are wet (with tears), until we see face to face the tender figure of the One, who says to us, "I am thy Father." [3] At this thought our hearts beat, even as when we behold the brilliant clouds in the evening sky or the pale moonlight of the fast-falling night. . . . Should any season be passed without thinking of the compassionate promise, "Constantly I am thinking of you"? [4] Should any month or day be spent without

[1] *Works*, pp. 469–476.
[2] Yam., p. 139; see below, p. 70.
[3] Yam., p. 473; Text, p. 326, line 7; SBE., p. 309.
[4] Yam., p. 473; Text, p. 326, line 11; SBE., p. 310.

revering the teaching that there is none who cannot attain Buddhahood? . . . Devote yourself whole-heartedly to the "Adoration to the Lotus of the Perfect Truth," and utter it yourself as well as admonish others to do the same. Such is your task in this human life.

It must not be ignored, however, that even this writing contains a sharp argument against the opponents of the Lotus.

Another instance of tenderness is shown in a letter[1] written to a lady who had asked about the rules to be observed during her monthly period. This was regarded by Japanese custom as a pollution, and women in this state were forbidden to approach Shinto sanctuaries. Her question, therefore, was, what she should do about the Scripture during that time. Nichiren deems it unnecessary to observe any precaution in that respect, and admonishes her to recite the Scripture as usual. Yet he adds that, if, because of the habit and custom, she has scruples about doing so, she need not hold the rolls of the Scripture; it will suffice to pronounce the Sacred Title. Delicate consideration and counsel of this kind are by no means rare in Nichiren's instructions, but they become more frequent after his return from exile. In general, we see how exile and residence among the simple country folk had tempered Nichiren's spirit, making him more gracious and sympathetic. His close contact with the people of Izu, especially the fisherman and his wife who sheltered him there, led him to give his instruction a more popular form and to take a deeper personal interest in his followers.

In the autumn of the following year (1264), while Nichiren was thus carrying on his propaganda, both polemic and persuasive, the illness of his mother called him to his native

[1] *Works*, pp. 477–485, dated the seventeenth of the fourth month (May 15) 1264.

place. When he arrived at home, his mother was seemingly dead. The pious son was, however, not disheartened, but went on to pray that her life might be restored. His prayer was heard, or his supernormal power proved efficacious, and gradually the aged mother recovered her health. Not only was his mother's restored health a great joy to Nichiren, but the demonstration of his miraculous powers led him at once to take a step toward the fulfilment of a pious desire long since cherished by him, the conversion of his old master Dōzen, the abbot of Kiyozumi, who still remained a believer in Amita and practised Shingon mysteries. The three objects of reverence and gratitude in Nichiren's religious ethics, as we shall see later, were a man's parents, ruler, and master. Nichiren's parents had long since been converted to his faith — the father had died six years before; but his efforts to convert the rulers were still unsuccessful, and his old master had never been subject to his influence, from the day of the first sermon in the assembly hall of Kiyozumi eleven years before. Nichiren now visited the abbot at a monastery in the country, explained his own conviction, expressed his pious desire for his master's conversion, exposed the old man's error, tenderly persuaded him to enter on the true way. But, alas! the man was now too old and weak to abandon the religious practices to which he had long been accustomed and become his former pupil's convert. He appreciated Nichiren's kindly intention, thanked him for his zeal, and wept with conflicting emotions; but the meeting was, after all, a failure. This remained a great regret to Nichiren throughout his life.[1]

This visit to his native place was an interlude in the perilous life of Nichiren; affectionate reminiscences of his

[1] After the old man's death, Nichiren, in 1276, still tried to mitigate this sorrow, by dedicating to the dead master a writing of spiritual admonition.

childhood were associated with a pious desire to perpetuate these early relationships to eternity. But the interlude was destined to be interrupted; wherever Nichiren, the apostle of the Truth, went, the shadow of danger attended him. The shadow now was embodied in the person of the local chief who had tried to kill him immediately after the assembly at Kiyozumi. When Nichiren parted from the abbot and left the village convent where they had met, his adversary was waiting for him. It was early in the evening on an autumn day[1] that Nichiren, accompanied by a few disciples from among the monks and some believing warriors, was making his way through the gloom of a pine forest. The pursuer, with hundreds of his troops cut off the way. The danger was imminent. "Shooting arrows flew like rain drops," Nichiren narrates,[2] "and the sparks from clashing swords were like lightning. One of my disciples was instantly killed, two others severely wounded, and I myself received a blow (on the forehead). There seemed to be no hope of escape, but I was saved — how, I cannot explain. Thus my gratitude toward the Lotus of Truth has ever since grown deeper." The wound on his forehead was left to remind him of his narrow escape. The orphan boy of the warrior disciple who had died in his defence became Nichiren's favorite disciple, and served the prophet with an inherited devotion.

Although the attack seems to have been prompted by diverse motives, Nichiren saw in it a plot organized by the Amita-Buddhists. It had the effect of confirming his conviction of the falsity of Amita-Buddhism, and the truth of his own religion; and, what was far more important, of

[1] The eleventh of the eleventh month, that is, December 1, 1264.

[2] *Works*, p. 524; in an epistle addressed to Lord Nanjō, about a month after the event. He refers to the incident in later writings in similar words.

strengthening the faith of Nichiren and his followers that he was a man sent and protected by the Lord Śākya-muni, and by his Truth. The belief in his mission which had been growing since his days in Izu reached a stage in which the self-consciousness of the prophet is more explicitly proclaimed. After having told of the incident, in the letter above cited, and quoting the same passages of the Scripture he cited in his writings in Izu, Nichiren tells more of himself.

> There are many in Japan who read and study the Lotus of Truth; there are, again, many who are attacked because they have conspired against others; but there is none who is abused because of (his revering) the Lotus of Truth. Thus, none of the men in Japan who hold to the Scripture have yet realized what is stated in the Scripture (since every one who really holds to it must encounter perils on that account); the one who really reads it is none other than I, Nichiren, who put in practice the text, " We shall not care for bodily life, but do our best for the sake of the incomparable Way." Then I, Nichiren, am the one, supreme one, the pioneer of the Lotus of Truth.[1]

Another interval, lasting nearly four years, followed the peril at the Pine Forest, and it was a fruitful period in Nichiren's harvest of converts! During these years Nichiren went on missionary journeys in the eastern provinces, and succeeded in converting many local lords. The first thing which strikes us in the results of his propaganda is that there were only a few among his disciples who had been Buddhist monks, and that most of his followers were recruited from among the warriors and feudal lords. Most of the warriors converted by him remained laymen and became the " outside " supporters of Nichiren; but they dedicated to the religion their brothers or sons who, after the years of their novitiate, were ordained, and worked under the master in disseminating his doctrine. The first converts made by

[1] A letter sent to Lord Nanjō, dated the thirteenth of the twelfth month (January 1, 1265). *Works*, p. 524.

Nichiren, as we mentioned, were his parents, who were given the Buddhist names Myōnichi and Myōren respectively, meaning " Perfection-Sun " and " Perfection-Lotus." The first monk disciple was Nisshō, who had been the master's fellow-student on Hiei, and had followed him to Kamakura. After this comes a list of converts from the warrior class, or their sons and brothers. During the four years of which we are now speaking, there was a notable increase in numbers, and it was in the years before and after Nichiren's exile to Izu that his religion was planted in the provinces of Awa and Kazusa, which have been its stronghold down to the present time.

This chapter may properly conclude with quotations from poems ascribed to the prophet on these missionary journeys.

Outside pours the rain, and its drops strike the windows.
Surely, it is not thy own nature, O rain, that makes thee fall aslant,[1]
But the wind that causes thee to beat so noisily on the sliding screens.

My body is all wet with the rain drops —
Nay, by my own tears, shed over calamities and perils;
And yet, under the " Umbrella-Forest " I am sheltered,
Now, even on this dreary evening.

These poems reflect the hardships he encountered everywhere, and make us vividly imagine a poor monk, clad in simple gray robes, with a little bag in his hands and a straw umbrella-hat on his head, passing stormy nights in cottages or deserted shrines. The latter of the poems cited is said to have been written in a shrine dedicated to Kwannon, at Kasa-mori, or " Umbrella-Forest," which stands today marking the site.

[1] The word rendered " nature " also means " conscience," and " aslant, oblique," means " crooked, vicious." Thus the didactic purpose of the verse is clear.

CHAPTER V

THE THREATENING MONGOL INVASION AND THE SENTENCE OF DEATH

WHILE Nichiren was warning the nation of the possible calamity of a foreign invasion, the Mongol conquerors of the Asiatic continent were preparing for an expedition to the eastern islands. The Korean peninsula had already been subjugated, but the Hōjō government did not yet fully realize the situation, although they must have had some knowledge of it. It is a question whether Nichiren had had any definite information when he wrote the warning essay in 1257–60.[1] At any rate, a panic was caused when, in 1268, an envoy from Kublai, the Mongol emperor, was reported to be proceeding to Japan by way of Korea. This embassy had not reached Japan; but it was a triumph for Nichiren, when, in 1268, another envoy urged a definite answer to the Khan's demand for the payment of tribute, and the government and the people realized the gravity of the situation. Nichiren now went back to Kamakura and renewed his appeal to the government. "Recall my prophetic warning given eight years ago! Is it not now being realized? Is there any man beside Nichiren who can repel this national danger? Only the one who knows the real cause of the situation can command it." Thus he argued.

[1] One theory is that Nichiren must have known the situation on the continent well enough, even early in the fifties, because while he was in Hiei, he had most probably made investigations about the feasibility of going to China as he desired. On the other hand, we know that the Chinese, Dōryu, Nichiren's bitterest opponent, came to Japan in 1246, and another Chinese in 1260.

As this appeal remained unanswered, the prophet determined to take more radical measures. After two months, he sent letters to the high officials of the government and to the abbots of the great monasteries, urging them to abandon their former faith and practices, and to adopt Nichiren's religion. There are eleven of these letters, each carrying its own special warning.

At the same time he sent a circular to his followers, in which he says: [1]

> In consequence of the arrival of the Mongol envoy, I have sent eleven letters to various officials and prelates. Prosecution will surely overtake Nichiren and his followers, and either exile or death will be the sentence. You must not be at all surprised. Strong remonstrances have intentionally been made, simply for the purpose of awakening the people. All is awaited by Nichiren with composure. Do not think of your wives and children and households; do not be fearful before the authorities! Make this your opportunity to sever the fetters of births and deaths, and to attain the fruit of Buddhahood! etc.

All these letters are dated the eleventh of the tenth month (November 16), 1268, eight months after the arrival of the Mongol envoy. We know nothing about the effect of the remonstrances, but there are indications that the government authorities summoned some of Nichiren's warrior followers, and examined their connection with Nichiren's propaganda. Meanwhile, Nichiren himself is believed to have left Kamakura, and to have been on missionary journeys, during about two years after this event. This silence and retirement, if they are real, seem to have been a period of preparation for another and decisive step, which he contemplated for the purpose of remonstrance and combat; and the psychological condition of Nichiren during this period may perhaps be compared to the retirement of Christ to Galilee before his last entry into Jerusalem. At any rate,

[1] *Works*, pp. 617–618.

toward the end of 1270, we again see Nichiren in Kamakura, and in a letter dated the twenty-eighth of the eleventh month (January 11, 1271), we read his resolution, as he was maturing his plans for the ensuing combat. It says: "I was once exiled on account of my cause, the Lotus of Truth. Something seems still to be lacking until I shall be executed. Wishing that this might happen, I sent strong remonstrances to various authorities. Now, my life has reached the fiftieth year. Why should I expect to live very much longer? Let me dedicate this life, with you, to the unique truth of the Lotus — the bodily life which is destined once finally to be abandoned in an uncultivated field."[1] In the following summer of 1271, we find him engaged in a contest with other Buddhists in a ritual against a drought. After this, events moved rapidly, leading to a sentence of death pronounced upon the aggressive prophet.

When Nichiren reappeared in Kamakura, the hatred of the rival Buddhists toward him was implacable. Especially Ryōkwan, the abbot of Gokuraku-ji and the greatest philanthropist of the time,[2] being incensed by Nichiren's fierce proclamation, charged him with disturbing the public order, and demanded a retraction from him. Nichiren defended himself against the charges, and challenged his opponent to a public debate. Ryōkwan was revered by the nobility and the people as the greatest teacher of Buddhist discipline, and was regarded as an incarnation of the Buddha Bhaiśājya-guru, or Medicine-master,[3] because of his care for the sick and infirm; and a man of such high position as the

[1] *Works*, p. 635.

[2] This man was the chief figure among those in whom Nichiren thought he found an embodiment of the opponents of the third category. See above, p. 41.

[3] A special manifestation of Buddha.

abbot of a monastery endowed by the government was deemed to be too dignified to enter a public debate with a beggar-like monk. Then in the summer the country suffered from a long drought, and when Ryōkwan's mystic ritual seemed to be fruitless to bring a rainfall, Nichiren vehemently accused the former of being a vain hypocrite. Intrigue against Nichiren was going on behind the scene among the court ladies of the Hōjō, who were all admirers of Ryōkwan. Public accusations were also made from various sides. At last, on the tenth of the ninth month (October 15, 1271), Nichiren was called into court to explain himself. He declared that his accusers were great liars, and repeated his warning about the imminent Mongol invasion, to the same effect as in his previous utterances. The man who was most offended and irritated was Hei no Saemon, the major-domo of the Hōjō, a fervent believer in Amita-Buddhism. Two days later, while the question was still pending in the court, Nichiren sent to him the essay, *Risshō Ankoku Ron*, together with a letter almost amounting to an ultimatum. The breach was too wide to be closed; the critical moment was at hand.

On the morning of the same day, the twelfth, probably while Nichiren's ultimatum was still on the way, a body of troops, led by the major-domo himself, surrounded Nichiren's hut. Nichiren stood on the veranda with the rolls of the Scripture in his hands. The soldiers hesitated to attack him, but he made no resistance. When the soldiers finally seized him, he loudly exclaimed, "Behold, the Pillar of Japan is now falling." He was tried before the Supreme Court on the charge of high treason. The judgment was immediately pronounced, and it seems to have been a sentence of banishment; but his life was left to the mercy of the custodian, Nichiren's opponent himself, Hei no Saemon — a method of disposing of cases not unusual in that age. In the evening, the prisoner was carried around on horseback in the city, and late in the night he was carried to Tatsu-no-kuchi, the Dragon's Mouth, the execution ground, about two miles from Kamakura. As he passed the Red Bridge in the middle of the town, he commanded the guard to stop. While the amazed soldiers obeyed and the crowd were wondering what was going to happen, the giant monk dismounted from the horse and stood facing north, toward the sanctuary of Hachiman. Hachiman, or the Eight-Banners Deity, was the patron god of the Minamotos, and a magnificent temple dedicated to him was erected at Kamakura when it was the seat of the Dictatorial government. It ever remained the holiest sanctuary of the military headquarters and the Dictator's residence. The Red Bridge was on the great avenue running through the middle of the city,[1] from the front of the Hachiman temple to the seashore. There the prisoner monk stood, and fixing his gaze on the seat of worship, spoke thus:

O Hachiman! Art thou really a divine being? When the Great Master Dengyō gave lectures on the Lotus of Truth, thou didst honor him by offering a purple robe. Now, I, Nichiren, am the one, the supreme one, who lives the life of the Lotus of Truth.[2] There is no fault in me, but I am proclaiming the Truth, simply in order to save all the people of this country from falling down to the nethermost hells because of their degrading the Lotus of Truth. Should the Mongols subjugate this country, wouldst thou, O Hachiman, together with the Sun-Goddess, alone be safe? Moreover, when our Lord Śākya-muni revealed the Lotus of Truth, all the Buddhas came together from the ten quarters; and when innumerable hosts, including the deities and saints of India, China, and Japan, were present in the congregation,

[1] Even today the temple and the avenue remain, almost as they were in the thirteenth century. The site of the Red Bridge is near the place where the railway viaduct crosses the central avenue of the city.

[2] This expression, "*Nippon dai-ichi no Hokke-kyō no gyōja*," in the original, has appeared before, and is used more frequently from this time on.

each of you took oath to guard those who should work to perpetuate the Truth. Now thou oughtest to come here and fulfil thy oath, and why dost thou not do it? . . . When, tonight, I, Nichiren, shall be beheaded and go to the Paradise of Vulture Peak, I shall declare before our Lord Śākya-muni that thou, Hachiman, and the Sun-Goddess have not fulfilled your oaths. Art thou not afraid of that? [1]

Then Nichiren mounted his horse and rode dignifiedly on. The soldiers and the crowd were amazed, and every one was questioning with himself, "Is he mad, or is he really a superman?" Superstitious awe was mingled with high admiration; pity and sympathy were displaced by the thought, "What extraordinary audacity! The sign of a supernatural power!"

Along the road on which Nichiren's guard proceeded many of his believers wept and cried, some of them daring even to approach him. He took farewell of them, either in silence or with a word of consolation. The faithful warrior, Kingo, together with his brothers, accompanied his master to the execution ground, and Nichiren later expressed his high appreciation of their fidelity unto death. Most of Nichiren's monk disciples had been arrested and imprisoned; and to them, after his miraculous escape from death, he wrote consoling letters.

It was some time past midnight when Nichiren arrived at Tatsu-no-kuchi. Everything was ready for his execution; soldiers surrounded the place; the official witness, Hei no Saemon, was sitting in a chair, the executioner standing behind. Nichiren sat down on a straw mat, joined his hands in worship, uttered the Sacred Title, and, stretching out his neck, awaited the stroke of the sword. Suddenly, and miraculously, as he himself and others believed, the sky was ablaze with light. "Something bright, like a ball of

[1] *Works*, pp. 1392–1393; written five years later, in 1276.

fire, flew from the southeast to the northwest, and every one's face was clearly visible in its light. The executioner became dizzy, and fell; soldiers were panic-stricken, some running away, others prostrate even on horseback."[1] Everything was in confusion, and the execution was no longer possible.

This narrow escape, more unexpected and miraculous than in any preceding cases, impressed Nichiren so deeply that he regarded his life thereafter as a second life—the life after a resurrection. In a later writing he expressed this thought as follows:[2]

> A man called Nichiren was beheaded at Tatsu-no-kuchi, a little after midnight of the twelfth day of the ninth month last year. His soul remained, and came here to the island of Sado; it wrote this, in the midst of snow, in the second month of the year following, and leaves it to posterity.

Another letter,[3] written in 1277 to his beloved warrior disciple Kingo, shows how gravely he regarded the crisis:

> Over and over I recall to mind that you came following me when I was going to be beheaded, and that you cried and wept, holding the bridle of my horse. How can I forget that as long as I may live? If you should fall to the hells because of your grave sins (accumulated in the past), I would not follow the call of my Lord Śākya, howsoever he might invite me to Buddhahood, but I would surely be in the hell where you are. If I and you are in the hells, Śākya Buddha and the Scripture will surely be there together with us.

Another letter addressed to the same warrior, written while the crisis was still fresh in his memory, says:[4]

> Tatsu-no-kuchi is the place where Nichiren renounced his life. The place is therefore comparable to a paradise; because all has taken

[1] *Works*, p. 1394.
[2] In the "Opening the Eyes." (*Works*, p. 804), written in 1272.
[3] *Works*, p. 1644; cp. p. 1812.
[4] Seven days after the event (*Works*, p. 690).

place for the sake of the Lotus of Truth. . . . Indeed every place where Nichiren encounters perils is Buddha's land. . . . Surely when I shall be on Vulture Peak, I shall inform our Lord of your fidelity shown in your readiness to follow me to death.

The authorities were perplexed what to do. When the day dawned, it was decided that the prisoner should be sent to Echi, a village fifteen miles inland from Tatsu-no-kuchi. When, at noon, he arrived there, he was received very reverently into the mansion of the local chief, and the soldiers of the guard began to listen to what the wonderful man said and preached. Meanwhile, it seems, the government circle were much disturbed by the failure of the execution, and a faction among the officials seems to have raised its voice against those who had urged that Nichiren should be put to death. Late in the following night a special messenger came from Kamakura, ordering that good care be taken of the prisoner. Finally, he was sentenced to exile, and, nearly a month later, he left Echi for the Island of Sado, which was designated as his place of banishment.

CHAPTER VI

THE EXILE IN SADO AND THE RIPENING OF NICHIREN'S FAITH IN HIS MISSION

TEN days were spent in the journey from the southern coast of Japan to the northern, and Nichiren now stood on the exposed coast of Echigo, gazing upon the waves raging in a winter gale. On the way thither he had travelled over hills and passes, crossed streams and valleys never before trodden by him. Now, in the midst of winter,[1] the lands all along the northern coasts were covered with snow. There he saw for the first time the Sea of Japan — this man who hitherto had known only the Pacific Ocean. The gale raged so continuously that he was obliged to stop at the little haven of Teradomari for a week. All of his past life seemed to him something like a series of frightful dreams, yet the dreams were as real as any facts of human life — nay, more real than anything else, because the records had been written in his tears and blood. During his stay there, while waiting to embark, he pondered over the past and the future. " Mountains beyond mountains " he had found in his journey in coming thither, and " waves upon waves " were raging in the sea before him. Similar had been his past experience, and such was also the prospect of the coming years. He examined and reviewed all the history of his life,

[1] He left Echi on the tenth day of the tenth month (November 13), arrived at Teradomari on the twenty-first day (November 24), wrote the letter quoted below on the following day, embarked for Sado on the twenty-seventh (November 30), landed there on the following day (December 1), and was installed in an abandoned hut on the first day of the eleventh month (December 4), 1271.

comparing it with the words of the Scripture, and could only arrive at the same conclusion he had come to in Izu, but now upon more conclusive evidence.

Although every step of his perilous life had been a subject of reflection in the light of the prophecies in the Scripture, Nichiren had never before had an opportunity so well suited to a comprehensive retrospect and profound meditation as at this time. As he reviewed it, his career had step by step fulfilled, almost to the letter, the prophecies concerning the propagators of the Truth; and now he was entering a new life, after a resurrection — the proper part of his life as the man wholly dedicated to the cause of the Truth, as well as to the spiritual welfare of all people in the coming days of degeneration. "The one, the pioneer, who lives the life of the Lotus of Truth," was surely not a product of chance, but a realization of the vows and promises recorded in the Scripture. Then, why should not he, Nichiren, be in vital continuity with some of those saints who had been commissioned by Buddha to work in the future, and were destined to suffer persecutions on that account? Many persons are mentioned who appeared in the assembly of the Lotus, and took the vows to perpetuate the Truth. Whoever they might be, Nichiren must be one of them — this was the conviction that was now firmly established in his mind. This is stated in a letter addressed to one of his earliest believers, Lord Toki, written one day after his arrival at Teradomari. This letter [1] is the first of a series of testimonies evincing Nichiren's consciousness that he was a reincarnation of one of the saints in the prophecies.

After a brief narrative of the journey, the letter quotes the passages to which Nichiren had paid special attention,

[1] *Works*, pp. 697–700; dated the twenty-second of the tenth month (November 25), at eight o'clock in the morning.

interpreting the meaning of his life. The quotations are similar, but in this letter a special emphasis is laid on passages in the thirteenth chapter on "Perseverance," such as, "They will deride us and abuse us, and assail us with weapons and sticks," "We shall repeatedly be driven out of our abodes." He continues:

> Nichiren has indeed been driven out repeatedly, and exiled twice. The Lotus of Truth proclaims the truths which are universal to all ages, past, present, and future. (What it says concerning the past is to be true of the present, and what it announces to occur in the present will be fulfilled again in the future.) Thus, the chapter on the Bodhisattva Sadāparibhūta,[1] telling what happened to him in the past, is now being realized in (the life of one who is practising) what the chapter on Perseverance tells, and *vice versa*. Then, surely (the man who is now realizing) the Perseverance will be in future (the man who practises the life of) Sadāparibhūta. Thus, Nichiren will be the Bodhisattva Sadāparibhūta. . . . (The chapter on Perseverance says that in the future, in the days of the Latter Law, there will appear eight billions of millions of saints who practise their vows.) Now, in these days there are the three kinds of opponents of the Truth (as exemplified in Nichiren's persecutors); and yet, if not one of those millions of saints should appear, it would be something as if an ebb were not followed by a flood; and as if the moon, when it had waned, did not wax again. When the water is clear, the moonlight is reflected in it; when a tree grows, birds abide in its branches. Nichiren is the vicar of those saints, eight billions of millions in number, and is protected by them all.

The vicar of the innumerable saints who took the vows of "Perseverance" was the Bodhisattva Sadāparibhūta. Nichiren is not here quite as definite as he was in a letter addressed to the same lord, more than one month later, from Sado. In the latter [2] he says, in part:

> During nearly two months since my arrival in this island of Sado, icy winds have been constantly blowing, and, though the snowfall is

[1] Chapter xx (Sanskrit Text, Chapter xix); see above, p. 30.

[2] *Works*, pp. 702–703; dated the twenty-third of the eleventh month (December 26), 1271.

sometimes intermitted, the sunlight is never seen. My body is penetrated by the cold, whereof (as is told concerning the cold hells) there are eight kinds . . . As I have written you, during the two thousand and two hundred years since Buddha's death, various masters have appeared in the world and labored to perpetuate the Truth, knowing its import, and yet adapting it to the needs of the times. The great masters Tendai and Dengyō made explicit the purport of the Truth (by uttering its Sacred Title), and yet they did not propagate it. One who shall fulfil this task is to appear in this country. If so, may not Nichiren be the man ? . . . The Truth has appeared and the omens are already more clearly manifest than ever before. The Scripture says, " There appeared four leaders, Viśiṣṭa-cāritra," etc.

This is the first definite statement[1] about his personal connection with Viśiṣṭa-cāritra (Jap. *Jōgyō*), the leader of the saints called out of earth in the chapter on the " Apparition of the Heavenly Shrine." From this time on, Nichiren remained constant in the belief that his former life was that of Viśiṣṭa-cāritra, although he often referred to other saints as his predecessors, and spoke as if he were a reincarnation of one of them.

The place where Nichiren was abandoned was a hut in a cemetery, little sheltered from wind and snow. No regular supply of food reached him. He was clad only in coarse hempen robes. It is a wonder how he survived these severities. He " felt in his body the eight kinds of icy cold," yet there was a fire in his inner heart; he almost starved, but he was provided with spiritual ambrosia. Yet he would have died of cold and hunger, if a zealous adversary, who at first attempted to kill him, had not been, contrary to his intention, converted by Nichiren. The man was a warrior who had come thither in attendance on the ex-emperor, who had been banished to the island more than fifty years before.

[1] A reference to the same man is made in the first essay after his return from Izu, (*Works*, p. 472), but is not directly referred to Nichiren himself.

He continued to live there, and was a devout Amita-Buddhist. The honest but simple-minded man, having heard of Nichiren's antagonism to Amita-Buddha, determined to kill the devil monk. He approached the solitary hut, and watched for an opportunity to stab the hated man, but was involuntarily attracted by Nichiren's voice as he recited the Scripture, and finally entered into religious discussion with him, because he thought it not proper for a Buddhist and a warrior to kill another without giving him warning and attempting to convert him. The man, no match in learning and piety for Nichiren, was converted by him whom he had formerly hated. His wife followed the example of her husband, and it was they who supplied Nichiren with food. They remained faithful to him until death; and, as in the case of the fisherman and his wife in Izu, the prophet never forgot to be grateful to them. Several tender letters written to them later are testimonies to the close relation established between the master and his converts. Hatred and persecution, on the one hand, but consolation and protection, both miraculous and human, on the other, all worked to strengthen Nichiren's gratitude toward the Scripture and his faith in his mission as the messenger of Buddha.

In this way the severest of the winter season was passed. Several communications were meanwhile received from Nichiren's followers on the mainland. By the time the snow and frost began to melt and the sun was pouring down its warm rays, the exile was no longer solitary and deserted, but had about him a few converts, and was preparing to continue his work. The work to be done was, of course, of quite a different sort from that which he had done in combating others. The fifty years before the " resurrection " were introductory to the proper part of his mission. There, in Sado, he was to arrive at the climax of his life, the revelation of the profound truth of his gospel. This idea was a necessary consequence of Nichiren's belief that his own life was an embodiment of the Lotus of Truth, because the Scripture was always divided by interpreters into three parts, the introduction, the climax, and the consummation and perpetuation.[1] Nichiren conceived his own mission in conformity with this division, and the task to be done in the climax of his life, now begun, was to reveal the essence of his religion, which in the event proved to be the revelation of the "Supreme Being" in a symbolic representation of the universe.

For this ultimate revelation he had to prepare the way, just as the revelation of the Tathāgata's infinite life (chapter xvi) had been preceded by the issuing of the innumerable hosts of the primeval disciples (chapter xv). These preparations consisted of a concise exposition of his doctrines, and of a critical estimate of the relative values of various religious and ethical systems. The exposition is contained in an essay entitled, "The Heritage of the Sole Great Thing Concerning Life and Death,"[2] together with a cognate essay on "The Oral Instruction for the Attainment of Buddhahood by Trees and Grasses."[3] After this, in the same month, was finished the "Opening the Eyes," Nichiren's greatest treatise on the ethical aspect of his religion, with reference to his own mission as well as to his followers' duties toward himself and Buddha. All these were com-

[1] Taken as a whole, the nineteen chapters from the second to the twentieth were regarded as the proper part, while in the two other divisions, the "manifest" part and the "primeval" part, the proper part of the former consisted of chapters ii–ix, and in the latter of xvi and a part of xvii.

[2] *Works*, pp. 742–744; written on the eleventh of the second month (March 12), 1272.

[3] *Works*, pp. 745–746; dated the twentieth (March 21).

pleted by the time the first winter in Sado was coming to an end, and, with the return of vernal breezes, the outlook was growing brighter. " Do even trees and grasses attain Buddhahood ? " you ask. " But the truth is, Buddha manifests himself as trees and grasses. The whole universe in its essence is nothing but Buddha's own body." In these utterances we can see the cosmological aspect of Nichiren's doctrine, as well as the surroundings in which the words were written down.

Now, let us see what is said concerning the Heritage of the Great Thing.

What I call the Heritage of the Great Thing Concerning Life and Death is nothing else than the Scripture, the Lotus of the Perfect Truth. For the Sacred Title of the Lotus was handed down from the two Buddhas, Śākya-muni and Prabhūta-ratna, to the Bodhisattva Viśiṣṭa-cāritra, when the Buddhas appeared in the Heavenly Shrine, and from eternity the heritage has been kept without interruption. " Perfect " represents death,[1] and " Truth," life; while life and death make up the essence of the ten realms of existence — the essence identical with that of the Lotus. . . . All that is born and dies is a birth and death of the Scripture (Truth), the Lotus in its ultimate reality. . . . Then, to utter the Sacred Title of the Lotus with the conviction that the three are one — the three, that is, Śākya-muni, the Buddha who from eternity has realized Buddhahood; the Lotus of Truth, which leads all beings, without exception, to Buddhahood; and we, beings in all the realms of existence. To utter the Sacred Title is, therefore, the Heritage of the Sole Great Thing Concerning Life and Death. This is the essential key to (the religious life of) Nichiren's disciples and followers, namely, adherence to the Lotus of Truth. . . .

Wherever Nichiren's disciples and followers utter the Adoration of the Lotus of the Perfect Truth — being united in heart, even in separate existences, like the association existing between fish and water,

[1] Nichiren interpreted the word " Perfect " (Sanskrit, *sad*) to mean resurrection, the mysterious continuity and perpetuity of life through births and deaths. In this sense death is but a phase in the perpetual flow of life, a step to another manifestation of life. Therefore, this interpretation. This thought of Nichiren's reminds us of Marcus Aurelius, when he said: Death, like birth, is a revelation of nature.

there, lies the Heritage of the Sole Great Thing Concerning Life and Death. This is the essence of what is promulgated by Nichiren. If it should be fulfilled, the great vow of propagating (the Truth throughout the Latter Days) over the whole world would be achieved. . . .

Will the Bodhisattva Viśiṣṭa-cāritra appear in these days of the Latter Law to open wide the gateway of the Truth, or will he not appear? The Scripture tells us so; yet will it surely happen? Will the Bodhisattva appear, or not? At any rate, I, Nichiren, have now accomplished the pioneer work.

Whatever may happen to you, arouse in yourselves a strong faith and pray that you may, at the moment of death, utter the Sacred Title in clear consciousness and with earnest faith! Do not seek besides this any heritage of the sole great thing concerning life and death. Herein lies the truth of the saying that there is Bodhi even in depravities, and Nirvāna even in birth and death.[1] Vain it is to hold the Lotus of Truth without this heritage of faith! I shall tell you more about this at another time. In sincerity and reverence.

Nichiren had passed through many perils, and was now going to reveal the kernel of his mission. For whose sake? Of course, for the sake of all beings living and going to live; but his vision was chiefly directed toward the future. Hence the "coming myriad of years" was the motto of his work. But could that task for the future be fulfilled without a remote cause and solid foundation laid in the past? All beings are to be saved. The task is grand and the end remote. The preparation for it must be proportionate to the magnitude of the future accomplishment. The necessary connection between the future and the past is shown in the revelation of the Heavenly Shrine, before which all primeval disciples of Buddha were summoned and took the vow to perpetuate the Truth throughout the coming ages. The link between the past and future is Nichiren,

[1] This does not mean to nullify the distinction between enlightenment and illusion, but to emphasize that truth is not to be sought beyond what we deem this life of vices and the realm of birth and death. The point may be seen in the synthesis of "vacuity" and "phenomenal reality," in the "Middle Path," for which see the Appendix.

who represents in this country at this moment the solemn pledge of salvation, and is commissioned to work in the days of degeneration. Thus his person is the key to the efficacious working of the everlasting Truth, which has its origin in eternity and is destined to prevail forever in the future.

This was Nichiren's conviction about his person and his mission. In order to open the eyes of all fellow-beings to this, it was necessary to bring them to the same enlightenment concerning themselves. For this purpose, each must, first of all, know the true relation existing between himself and the eternal Buddhahood, which is represented, preeminently, by the Lord Śākya, and is to be realized in one's own self. This metaphysical relation between the Master and the disciples, between the cosmos and the individual, is the very foundation of all religion and ethics. Open the eyes to this cardinal relation, then all enlightenment will naturally follow.

"There are three objects which every man ought to revere, his lord, his master, and his parents; there are three subjects which should be studied, Confucianism, Hinduism, and Buddhism." Thus begins the essay on "Opening the Eyes."[1] The key-note — the emphasis on the eternal Buddhahood — runs through all the argument, but the melody varies, just as diverse systems of religion and ethics are engaged in inculcating one and the same principle of reverence to the same objects of veneration. According to Nichiren, the manifold teachings existing are but the varying aspects of the same cosmic principle; and each of those systems represents a certain truth, while errors come from sticking to a particular point of the teachings. The Truth is touched, but the whole Truth is missed,

[1] *Works*, pp. 747–824; finished in the second month (March), 1272.

as squinting eyes, though not totally blind, distort images. The full-opened eyes see the Truth of the everlasting relationship between ourselves and the eternal Buddhahood, in which the Buddha, as revealed in the chapter on the Eternal Life of the Tathāgata, is the Lord ruling over all subjects, the Master leading his pupils to maturity, and the Father who gives birth to the children. We are, from all eternity, subjects of the Buddha, his disciples, and his children; being essentially like him through the eternal Truth. When seen in this light, every religion and ethical system, compared with Nichiren's religion revealed in the Lotus, is one of the preliminary steps leading up to the ultimate truth. Yet men are blind or squinting and do not see the whole truth in its full light.

Confucianism, being a system of humanitarian ethics, limits its view of this relationship to the visible side of human life. Hinduism, worshipping Brahmā or Vishnu as the highest Lord, goes a little beyond the actual world, yet sees in those phantom gods the ultimate Being. There are relative merits in these systems, but, after all, they are blind or half blind to the true foundation of human relations and religious worship. Buddhism opens our spiritual eyes to the being of Buddha, our Lord, yet many Buddhists are too "squint-eyed" to see his real nature and our proper relation to him. Nichiren criticizes these distorted forms of Buddhism most severely, and shows less clemency toward them than toward other religions. Especially Hīnayāna, the way of those who are contented with mere knowledge of certain truths or with solipsistic transcendence in contemplation, is further away from the true way than the secular teachings of ethics which inculcate loyalty and filial piety.

That Nichiren emphasized these virtues, together with obedience to the master, is noteworthy as showing his keen interest in moral life. It must be observed, also, that this ethical interest was not with him merely an adjunct of religious belief, but a vital criterion of religious truth. For to worship Buddha and revere the Truth revealed by him does not consist in devising rituals, or in contemplating Buddha's truths in visionary ways, but in working out in our own life the truths taught, by putting faith in Buddha as the Lord, Master, and Father. Faith ought to be actualized in life, but is empty unless realized in the three cardinal virtues named above. Nichiren's conviction that his life was vitalizing the Lotus of Truth was another way of stating his ethical interpretation of religion.

Buddha, as he is represented as declaring himself in the chapter on Eternity, is the Tathāgata from all eternity and has ever been working to lead all sentient beings to maturity in Buddhahood. He is the Lord of Truth and Father of all, and we are his disciples and children. Religion is nothing but the way to enlightenment in this eternal relationship, and morality, nothing but the method of realizing the same truth in our life. We have ever been Buddha's children, but, up to the present, we have been blind to his presence and work, just like the prodigal son in the parable in the fourth chapter of the Scripture. We are now awake to this everlasting fundamental relationship, and thereby shall surely attain Buddhahood, because the Tathāgata is constantly caring for us and watching over us, as he says:

> Now, this threefold realm of existence is my dominion,
> And all beings therein are my children.
> Yet existence is full of troubles and tribulations,
> I alone am the protector and savior.[1] (Chap. III).

[1] Verse 87; Text, p. 90; SBE., p. 88.

Since I have attained Buddhahood, . . .
I have constantly been preaching truths,
And helping innumerable beings to maturity,
Leading them in the Way of Buddhas;
Thus, innumerable aeons have passed in this work.[1] (Chap. XVI).

The duties of the true Buddhist, then, consist in fully knowing the vast scheme of Buddha's salvation working upon us, in being convinced of our indebtedness to Buddha, and in requiting it by practising the true morality.

Morality in human relation means, according to this point of view, a life of gratitude shown in fidelity to the Lord, obedience toward one's master, and filial piety toward one's parents; all other moral relations flow out of these fundamental ones. But this passive aspect of morality implies the active duty of showing gratitude by perpetuating the will of the benefactor. The ruled fulfills his duty by co-operating with the ruler in the maintenance of order and government, the disciple by propagating the truth taught by the master, and the child by perpetuating the life given by his parents. Similarly with moral duties viewed from the standpoint of religion: the true faith consists in propagating the Truth, and in ourselves living the life of Truth as revealed by Buddha. This is what is inculcated in the Scripture, and is the real import of the vows taken by the saints, the faithful disciples of Buddha.

The question for Nichiren, was, therefore, Is there any one, in the present age of degeneration, who practises the true essence of the Buddhist religion ? In order to answer this question, Nichiren proceeds anew to re-examine the stanzas of the chapter on Perseverance. The three kinds of opponents, the malicious laymen, the perverse monks, and

[1] Verses 1–2; Text, p. 323; SBE., p. 307.

the jealous hypocrites, have been actually embodied in Nichiren's persecutors. The persecutions heaped upon him are letter by letter prophesied in the Scripture; the perils which the saints, consecrating themselves, promised Buddha to endure—abuse and derision, weapons and sticks, banishment and execution — these have all been experienced in Nichiren's life. Is there, then, any room to doubt that Nichiren is the true Buddhist, the man who is realizing the prophecies about the propagator of the Truth in the Latter Days? If Buddha is really omniscient and his prophecies not falsehood; if the "Saints-out-of-Earth" are not liars and hypocrites, and their vows not vain; then Nichiren is surely the man who is fulfilling the vows of the old saints. Buddha is the primeval master, and Nichiren is now living the life of his primeval disciples. Primeval, therefore everlasting, and as true for the future as in the past — he is the one predestined to be the leader, the savior of the coming ages. In short, Nichiren is the man who is "reading" the Truth by his life.

By such considerations, Nichiren justified himself in his polemic attitude. The precedence he gives to the "repressive" method in propaganda over the "persuasive" was the necessity of the time; it was the way ordained by Buddha, because the malicious men of the Latter Days could be converted only by arousing their utmost malice, and thereby exterminating their radical sins.[1] Let men's eyes be opened to the existence and work of the true Buddha, and to the duties of the true Buddhist, and their sight will be clear enough to see in Nichiren the predestined manifestation

[1] The idea is that radical sin can be exterminated only by arousing the sinful thought and deed to the utmost. Nichiren compares the "repressive" method to a surgical operation, without which certain kinds of disease cannot be cured. Later, we shall see more of his idea of sin.

of the primeval saint, the messenger of the Tathāgata. Expressing this thought with firm confidence, Nichiren says:[1]

> Finally, let the celestial beings withdraw their protection, let all perils come upon me, even so, will I dedicate my life to this cause. . . . Be it in weal, be it in woe, to desert the Lotus of Truth means to fall to the hells. I will be firm in my great vow. Let me face all manner of threats and temptations. Should one say to me, "Thou mightest ascend the throne of Japan, if thou wouldst abandon the Scripture and expect future bliss through belief in the 'Meditation on Amita'; or thy parents shall suffer capital punishment, unless thou utterest the name of the Buddha Amita," etc. Such temptations I shall meet unshaken, and shall never be allured by them, unless my principles be shattered by a sage's refutation of them. Any other perils shall be the dust before a storm. I will be the Pillar of Japan; I will be the Eyes of Japan; I will be the Great Vessel of Japan.[2] Inviolable shall remain these oaths!

When Nichiren had finished the "Opening the Eyes," amidst the snows of winter, with the coming of the spring a better time began for him. The governor of the island was much attracted by his saintly life, as well as by his strong personality. The government issued an order to protect the exile; Nichiren was given an abode at Ichi-no-sawa, a place on the slope of a range of hills. The local chief of this region admired and protected him, showing him great respect; his wife and son were converted. The place of exile became a veritable centre of propaganda, and many flocked to listen to the sermons of the wonderful man. Nichiren reviewed his past experience anew, in calm reflection; the hardships he had gone through appeared in another light, and he now recognized that they were all in expiation of the grave sins accumulated from eternity through neglect or abandonment of duty, or through not having always lived as the true Buddhist. The strenuous repression of which he made so

[1] In the "Opening the Eyes," *Works*, p. 816.

[2] The Pillar means the supporter, the lordship; the Eyes, the mastership; and the Great Vessel, the giver of life, the fatherhood.

much in his combative propaganda meant the repression not only of others' illusions and vices, but of his own. In a letter[1] written about one month after the "Opening the Eyes," he sums up the arguments expounded in that work, and speaks of himself as follows:

That Nichiren suffers so much is not without remote causes. As is explained in the chapter on the Bodhisattva Sadāparibhūta, all abuses and persecutions heaped upon the Bodhisattva were the results of his previous karma. How much more, then, should this be the case with Nichiren, a man born in the family of an outcast fisherman, so lowly and degraded and poor! Although in his soul he cherishes something of the faith in the Lotus of Truth, the body is nothing but a common human body, sharing beastlike life, nothing but a combination of the two fluids, pink and white, the products of flesh and fish. Therein the soul finds its abode, something like the moon reflected in a muddy pool, like gold wrapped up in a dirty bag. Since the soul cherishes faith in the Lotus of Truth, there is no fear even before (the highest deities, such as) Brahmā and Indra; yet the body is an animal body. Not without reason others show contempt for this man, because there is a great contrast between the soul and the body. And even this soul is full of stains, being the pure moonlight only in contrast to the muddy water; gold, in contrast to the dirty bag.

Who, indeed, fully knows the sins accumulated in his previous lives? . . . The accumulated karma is unfathomable. Is it not by forging and refining that the rough iron bar is tempered into a sharp sword? Are not rebukes and persecutions really the process of refining and tempering? I am now in exile, without any assignable fault; yet this may mean the process of refining, in this life, the accumulated sins (of former lives), and being thus delivered from the three woeful resorts. . . .

The world is full of men who degrade the Lotus of Truth, and such rule this country now. But have I, Nichiren, not also been one of them? Is that not due to the sins accumulated by deserting the Truth? Now, when the intoxication is over, I stand here something like a drunken man who having, while intoxicated, struck his parents, after coming to himself, repents of the offence. The sin is hardly to be expiated at once. . . . Had not the rulers and the people persecuted me, how could I have expiated the sins accumulated by degrading the Truth?

[1] Sent to his disciples on the mainland; written on the twentieth of the third month (April 19), 1272. *Works*, p. 827–835.

Such reflections on his own sinfulness naturally led Nichiren to apply the same principles to his followers. No one is totally destitute of Buddha-nature, which is dormant in the innermost recess of the soul; but none is free from the sin of having disregarded and disobeyed the Truth. Nichiren is now fulfilling the oaths taken before Buddha, and thereby expiating his sins through a severe discipline in hardships. Persecutions are necessary accompaniments of the lives of those who labor for the sake of the Truth, because of their efforts to stir up the malicious and perverse nature of their fellow-beings, among whom the work of propagating the Truth is done. But the perils are at the same time a means of expiating the workers' own grave sins. Moreover, an existence of any kind is never an individual matter, but always the result of a common karma, shared by all born in the same realm of existence. Hence the expiation made by any one individual is, in fact, made for the sake of all his fellow-beings. Both the persecutors and the persecuted share the common karma accumulated in the past, and therefore share also in the future destiny, the attainment of Buddhahood. Nichiren's repression of others' malice and vice is at the same time his own expiation and self-subjugation. How, then, should his followers not share his merit in extinguishing the accumulated sins, and preparing for the realization of the primeval Buddha-nature? "Therefore," Nichiren exhorts his disciples, "believe in me, and emulate my spirit and work, in the firm faith that the Master is the savior and leader! Work together, united in the same faith! Then, the expiation of sins will be achieved for ourselves and for all our fellow-beings, because we all share in the common karma."

CHAPTER VII

THE CLIMAX OF NICHIREN'S LIFE; GRAPHIC REPRESENTATION OF THE SUPREME BEING

A PEACEFUL summer had passed, the short days of autumn followed one another, and the dreary winter was nigh. The exile continued to ponder on his mission, now more deeply and calmly than ever before. His faith in his mission was firmly established, and his aggressive propaganda was bearing fruit, not only in winning many converts, but even in inspiring awe in his opponents. Toward the end of the year in which he was banished, the Mongols caused fresh alarm by sending a number of ships, which were followed in the next year by another embassy. Family strife broke out among the Hōjōs, and members of the clan killed one another. All these events were interpreted by Nichiren and his followers as the results of the injustice done the prophet, and also as a fulfilment of his warning predictions. This was a triumph for Nichiren, but what concerned him more was the future of the nation and of the religion. In the Sacred Title he had given his religion a standard and a form of worship suitable to every people in the Latter Days; he had also explained who Buddha is, and the relation between Buddha and ourselves. But the object of worship had not yet been clearly defined. What should it be ? How should it be presented to men's physical and spiritual vision ? The next task, the consummation of his activities hitherto, was the solution of this problem, the revelation of the Supreme Being, and a preparation for the complete fulfilment of his great mission.

The thought had occupied him, as he tells us, since the autumn (eleventh month) of 1272. The way in which he solved the problem was quite characteristic of his philosophical cast of mind, as well as of his practical nature — philosophical, because Nichiren always emphasized the Truth, the metaphysical basis of existence, and was never content to worship a personal god, whether Buddha or any other deity, merely as a being existing beside ourselves; practical, because his special endeavor was to seize the very quintessence of Truth, and to present it in a way so simple and concrete that even the least intelligent might be inspired and moved by it.

Surely, the Lord Śākya-muni, when understood as the primeval Tathāgata, is the ultimate entity of the universe, and consequently the object of worship. Yet, when he is simply represented, as he is represented by other Buddhists, in an image, or in any other manner suggesting a particular person, the erroneous conception immediately arises, that the person is different from the Truth which he embodies. On the other hand, Nichiren's religion was not the worship of an abstract truth, but a life to be lived by every being, human, or other. Thus, the thing to be done was to unite the Truth and the Person in a concrete representation, and to regard it as the embodiment of the Supreme Being. This had been partly accomplished in the formula of worship symbolized in the Sacred Title. But this latter means of religious worship, chiefly intended for oral utterance, was to be supplemented by providing the soul with a representation of the Supreme Being which symbolized a perfect union of the eternal Truth with the primeval person of Buddha. The result was set forth in the "Spiritual Introspection of the Supreme Being," an essay finished on the twenty-fifth of the fourth month (May 13);[1] and a tangible symbolic representation was made on the eighth day of the seventh month (August 21), 1273. Now let us see what the idea and representation were.

The fundamental teaching of the Lotus concerning the reality of the universe amounts to this, that every being exists and subsists by virtue of the inexhaustible qualities inherent in each. There are innumerable individuals, and also groups of beings, including Buddhas and Bodhisattvas, celestial beings, mankind, furious spirits, beings in the purgatories, etc. Their respective characteristics are unmistakably distinct, but their qualities and conditions are constantly subject to change, because in each of the beings are inherent the qualities manifest in others, the differences arising simply from the varying configuration of the manifest and the potential qualities. Moreover, even taking the existences as they are at a given moment, they cannot subsist but by mutual interaction and influence. To subsist by itself by no means signifies to be separate from others; on the contrary, to interact one with another is the nature of every particular being. These features of existence are the laws or truths (*dharma*), and the cosmos is the stage of the infinite varieties and interactions of the *dharmas*, in other words, the realm of "mutual participation."[2]

These teachings are stated in the Lotus of Truth, and have been explained and elucidated by many a great master of the past; but they remain simply doctrines, so long as they are merely understood, and not personally experienced. Vain is all talk and discussion concerning existences and reality, unless the virtues of existence are realized in one's own person. Noble and sublime may be the conception of

[1] *Works*, pp. 928–949. [2] For these doctrines, see Appendix.

the Supreme Being, but it is but an idol or image, a dead abstraction, if we ourselves do not participate in its supreme existence and realize in ourselves its excellent qualities. Thus, worship or adoration means a realization of the Supreme Being, together with all its attributes and manifestations, first, through our own spiritual introspection, and, second, in our life and deeds. The practice of introspection is carried on in religious meditation. This, however, does not necessarily mean intricate and mysterious methods, such as are employed by many Buddhists; the end can be attained by uttering the Sacred Title, and by gazing in reverence at the graphic representation of the Supreme Being as revealed by Nichiren. The truths of universal existence and "mutual participation" remain abstractions if detached from the true moral life; but any morality, however perfect it may seem, is vain apart from the profound conviction in the truth of the "mutual participation," and from an apprehension of our primeval relation to the Lord of the Universe.

Thus, to participate in the virtues of the Supreme Being is the aim of worship; but that participation means nothing but the restoration of our primeval connection with the eternal Buddha, which is equivalent to the realization of our own true nature. In other words, the true self of every being is realized through full participation in the virtues of the Supreme Being, who, again, reveals himself—or itself—in the perfect life of every believer. The relation between the worshipped and the worshipper exemplifies most clearly the truth of "mutual participation," because the worshipped, the Supreme Being, is a mere transcendence if it does not reveal itself in the believer's life, while the worshipper realizes his true being and mission only through the elevating help (*adhiṣṭāna*) of the Supreme Being. Thus, mutual participation is at the same time mutual revelation — realization of the true being through mutual relationship, to be attained by us through spiritual introspection and moral living. Religious worship, in this sense, is at the same time moral life; and moral relationships in the human world are nothing but partial aspects of the fundamental correlation between us and the Supreme Being. The point to be emphasized in regard to this conception of the religious relation is that the Supreme Being alone, without our worship of it in enlightenment and life, is not a perfect Being, just as, without a child, "father" is but an empty name, if not a contradiction in terms.

With these thoughts on the truth of mutual revelation, and with a special emphasis on the necessity of a simple and concrete representation of the Supreme Being, Nichiren composed the treatise on "The Spiritual Introspection of the Supreme Being, Revealed for the First Time in the Fifth Five Centuries after the Tathāgata's Great Decease." He describes the symbolic representation as follows: [1]

The august state of the Supreme Being (*Svādi-devatā*) is this: The Heavenly Shrine is floating in the sky over the Sahā world [2] ruled by the Primeval Master, the Lord Buddha. In the Shrine is seen the Sacred Title of the Lotus of the Perfect Truth, on either side of which are seated the Buddhas Śākya-muni and Prabhūta-ratna, and also on the sides, at a greater distance, the four Bodhisattva leaders, the Viśiṣṭa-cāritra and others. The Bodhisattvas like Manjuśri and Maitreya are seated farther down, as attendants of the former, while the innumerable hosts of the Bodhisattvas, enlightened by the manifestations of Buddha, sit around the central group, like a great crowd of people looking up toward the court nobles surrounding the throne.

[1] *Works*, p. 940.

[2] A name for the world, as the abode of mankind. For Nichiren's idea of the world as a paradise, see below, pp. 104, 106–108.

In his graphic representation of this scene, Nichiren makes place for all other kinds of beings, men and gods, spirits and demons, all surrounding the central Sacred Title. His idea was to represent adequately, from his point of view, the perfect union of the Truth and the Person, manifested not only in Buddhas and saints, but inherent even in the beings immersed in illusion and vice. The whole was intended to be a visible embodiment of the truth of cosmic existence, as realized in the all-comprehensive conception of " mutual participation, and illuminated by the all-enlightening power of the Truth."

The universe is the stage of mutual participation and reciprocal interaction, which proceed according to the truths, or laws, of existence. Buddha, in his real entity, is nothing but another name for this cosmos of orderly existence. Seen from this angle, the Truth is fundamental and the Person is secondary; but the Truth and its laws cannot exist nor work without everlasting wisdom, the cosmic soul which is the source of all wisdom, which ordains all laws and causes all beings to exist. This is the personal aspect of the universe, and is the real personality of the eternal Buddha. Buddha, the Lord of Truth, as he declares himself to be, in the second chapter of the Lotus, and the eternal Father of the world, as he reveals himself in the sixteenth chapter, is the Father and Master of all beings. This Buddha has appeared, as is made known in the chapter on the Apparition of the Heavenly Shrine, in the person of two Buddhas, Śākya-muni and Prabhūta-ratna; and this celestial manifestation was meant to show the efficacy of Buddha's wisdom to lead all beings alienated from it to the full enlightenment of the universal truths. The basic truth of existence and its everlasting laws are inherent in every being, while the personal manifestations of Buddhahood are working to bring all beings to full consciousness of their own real nature. In other words, all beings, participating in the primeval wisdom of the universe, are developing their proper nature in conjunction with the educative activity of the Buddhas. Taking this view of the cosmic movement, the Supreme Being is nothing but the union of the Truth and the Person, as realized in the person of Buddha and to be realized in each of us.

This union is now graphically represented in the Cycle, or *Maṇḍala*, in the centre of which the Truth stands, surrounded by all kinds of existences. And the Cycle is the means to inspire our spiritual life with the truth of mutual interaction, and to induce us to full participation in the universal harmony. Seen in this light, the object of worship, the Supreme Being is to be sought nowhere but in the innermost recess of every man's nature, because the final aim of worship is the complete realization of the Supreme Being in ourselves. Ethically speaking, Buddha is our Lord and Father, but metaphysically the Lord and Father is the means of perpetuating Truth and Life, which are to be made actual by us. These two sides are united in the act of religious worship, which is, on the one hand, adoration of the universal Truth embodied in the person of Buddha, and, on the other, the realization, in thought and life, of the Buddha-nature in ourselves. These principles of ethical, metaphysical, and religious teaching were formulated by Nichiren in a further exposition of the conception of the Supreme Being, in the essay on "The Reality as It Is,"[1] written in the fifth month (June), that is, between the composition of the "Spiritual Introspection" and the revelation of the graphic representation in the *Maṇḍala*.

[1] *Works*, pp. 958–964.

This conception of the Buddha-nature, and of its realization in ourselves through worship, are consequences of the time-honored theory of the Threefold Personality (*tri-kāya*) of Buddha. But the characteristic feature in Nichiren's ideas is that he never was content to talk of abstract truth, but always applied the truth taught to actual life, bringing it into vital touch with his own life. Ethics and metaphysics are never to be separated, but to be united in religion, and religion means a life actually embodying truth and virtue. Truths are revealed and virtues inculcated in the Lotus of Truth, and consequently the true religious life is equivalent to " reading the Scripture by person." Thus, the essay, which begins with discussions of the metaphysical entity of Buddha-nature, proceeds naturally to a consideration of the Buddhist life, especially as exemplified in Nichiren's own life. In it he says: [1]

I, Nichiren, a man born in the ages of the Latter Law, have nearly achieved the task of pioneership in propagating the Perfect Truth, the task assigned to the Bodhisattva Viśiṣṭa-cāritra. The eternal Buddhahood of Śākya-muni, as he revealed himself in the chapter on Life-duration, in accordance with his primeval entity; the Buddha Prabhūta-ratna, who appeared in the Heavenly Shrine, in the chapter on its appearance, and who represents Buddhahood in the manifestation of its efficacy; the Saints (Bodhisattvas) who sprang out of the earth, as made known in the chapter on the Issuing out of Earth — in revealing all these three,[2] I have done the work of the pioneer (among those who perpetuate the Truth); too high an honor, indeed, for me, a common mortal! . . .

I, Nichiren, am the one who takes the lead of the Saints-out-of-Earth. Then may I not be one of them? If I, Nichiren, am one of them, why may not all my disciples and followers be their kinsmen? The Scripture says, " If one preaches to anybody the Lotus of Truth,

[1] *Works*, pp. 959–964.

[2] Nichiren meant the threefold aspects of Buddhahood, *Dharma-kāya*, the eternal essence of Buddha Śākya-muni, *Sambhoga-kāya*, the blissful manifestation in the person of Buddha Prabhūta-ratna, and *Nirmāna-kāya*, the condescension and actual working of the Bodhisattvas.

even just one clause of it, he is, know ye, the messenger of the Tathāgata, the one commissioned by the Tathāgata, and the one who does the work of the Tathāgata."[1] How, then, can I be anybody else than this one? . . .

By all means, awaken faith by seizing this opportunity! Live your life through as the one who embodies the Truth, and go on without hesitation as a kinsman of Nichiren! If you are one in faith with Nichiren, you are one of the Saints-out-of-Earth; if you are destined to be such, how can you doubt that you are the disciple of the Lord Śākya-muni from all eternity? There is assurance of this in a word of Buddha, which says: "I have always, from eternity, been instructing and quickening all these beings."[2] No attention should be paid to the difference between men and women among those who would propagate the Lotus of the Perfect Truth in the days of the Latter Law. To utter the Sacred Title is, indeed, the privilege of the Saints-out-of-Earth. . . .

When the Buddha Prabhūta-ratna sat in the Heavenly Shrine side by side with the Tathāgata Śākya-muni, the two Buddhas lifted up the banner of the Lotus of the Perfect Truth, and declared themselves to be the Commanders (in the coming fight against vice and illusion). How can this be a deception? Indeed, they have thereby agreed to raise us mortal beings, to the rank of Buddha. I, Nichiren, was not present there in the congregation, and yet there is no reason to doubt the statements of the Scripture. Or, is it possible that I was there? Common mortal that I am, I am not well aware of the past, yet in the present I am unmistakably the one who is realizing the Lotus of Truth. Then in the future I am surely destined to participate in the communion of the Holy Place. Inferring the past from the present and the future, I should think that I must have been present at the Communion in the Sky. (The present assures the future destiny, and the future destiny is inconceivable without its cause in the past.) The present, future, and past cannot be isolated from one another.

When I meditate on these things, my joy has no limit, in spite of the miseries of the life of an exile. Tears in joy, tears in afflictions. . . . I shed tears in thinking of the present perils and sufferings; my tears cannot be checked even in the midst of rejoicing over the destiny of Buddhahood that is before me. Birds and insects cry and weep, but shed no tears; I, Nichiren, neither cry nor weep, yet no moment passes without tears. These are shed, indeed, not on account of any worldly matter but for the sake of the Lotus of Truth. If this be so, these tears are drops of ambrosia. . . .

[1] Yam., p. 321; Text, p. 227, line 1; SBE., p. 216.

[2] Yam., p. 445; Text, p. 310, verse 43; SBE., p. 293.

In this document, the truths most precious to me are written down. Read, and read again; read into the letters and fix them into your mind! Thus put faith in the Supreme Being, represented in a way unique in the whole world! Ever more strongly I advise you to be firm in faith, and to be under the protection of the threefold Buddhahood. March strenuously on in the ways of practice and learning! Without practice and learning the Buddhist religion is nullified. Train yourself, and also instruct others! Be convinced that practice and learning are fruits of faith! So long as, and so far as, there is power in you, preach, if it be only a clause or a word (of the Scripture)! *Namu Myōhō-renge-kyō! Namu Myōhō-renge-kyō!* Sincerely, in reverence.

Let me add: Herewith I have delivered to you the truths revealed to me, Nichiren. Precious truths are specially transmitted to you. What a mysterious dispensation! . . . O, may I, Nichiren, be a kinsman of the Saints-out-of-Earth, six myriads of Gangā-sands in number? All this I do with the sole aim of leading all men and women in this country, Japan (nay in the world), to the communion of those who utter "*Namu Myōhō-renge-kyō.*" Does not the Scripture say, "The one called Viśiṣṭa-cāritra . . . and he, (together with the three other leaders) is the leader in utterance?"[1] That you have become my disciple is indeed the result of a remote connection. Keep this letter carefully for yourself! Know that I, Nichiren, have therein recorded the truths realized personally by myself! Good-by.[2]

The above essays were the introduction to the revelation of the Supreme Being in graphic representation. When he had thus expounded his thoughts, he undertook, in the summer of 1273, the work of the "revelation," the climax of his life work. The design was as described above, and beneath were added two postscripts. On the right side, "This is the great *Maṇḍala*, which has never before appeared throughout the whole Jambu-dvīpa (world) during the two thousand

[1] Yam., p. 431; Text, p. 300, lines 13–15; SBE., p. 284.

[2] The import of the treatise is further expanded, on its practical side, in the "*Nyosetsu-Shugyō-shō*," or "(Religious) Practice in Accordance with the Statements of the Scripture," written in the same month; in its metaphysical aspect, in the "*Tōtai-gi-shō*," or "Doctrine of the Entity," finished in the autumn of the same year. Between these, on the eleventh of the fifth month (May 28), was written the "*Ken-Butsu-mirai-ki*" or the "Realization of Buddha's Prophecies," which is cited below.

two hundred and twenty and more years elapsed since Buddha's decease." On the left side, "Having been sentenced (to death) on the twelfth day of the ninth month, in the eighth year of Bunnei, and having been later exiled afar to the island of Sado, on the eighth day of the seventh month, in the tenth year of the same, Nichiren makes this representation, for the first time."

Whatever Nichiren's followers may claim about this *Maṇḍala* and the postscripts, and whatever criticism modern scholars may make, it remains an undoubted fact that Nichiren attached the greatest importance to this work, as being the pivotal point in his life. After this, begins the last part of his life, the consummation, and preparation for the perpetuation, of his religion, in accordance with the threefold division of the Scripture mentioned above.

Let me conclude this chapter by quoting another letter, written at the same time with the "Reality as It Is." It is entitled "The Realization of Buddha's Prophecies,"[1] and is an additional witness to Nichiren's firm conviction of his mission.

What a great fortune it is to extinguish in this life the sins we have accumulated from eternity by degrading the Truth! What a joy to serve the Lord Śākya-muni, whom we had thought never to see or hear! Let these be my earnest desires, first of all, to persuade the rulers who have persecuted me, to announce to the Lord Śākya (the names of those) of my followers who have assisted me; and to recommend the highest good to my parents, who gave me birth, before they die.[2]

I have seen, as in a vision, the spirit of the "Apparition of the Heavenly Shrine." The text says,[3] "To grasp the world-mountain, Sumeru, and to throw it to the innumerable lands of Buddhas in

[1] *Works*, pp. 973–978.

[2] His parents had died before this time; but Nichiren spoke, not simply for himself, but for all his followers.

[3] Yam., pp. 360–361; Text, p. 253; SBE., p. 240.

various directions — even this is not a thing impossible; but a thing most difficult would it be adequately to preach the Scripture in the degenerate ages after Buddha's decease," etc.

The Great Master Dengyō said: "Śākya-muni has shown a clear distinction between the shallow, which is easy to grasp, and the profound, which is difficult to receive; and it should be the ambition of a great man, leaving the shallow, to take up the profound. The Great Master Tendai promulgated, in obedient faith in Lord Śākya, the doctrines of the Lotus of Truth in the land of Cathay; and our school, having its centre at Hiei, is doing the same in Japan, in accordance with the tradition of Tendai, for the sake of the Lotus of Truth."

I, Nichiren, a native of Awa, am most probably the man whose mission it is, succeeding to the heritage of the three masters, to propagate the doctrines of the Lotus of Truth throughout the ages of the Latter Law. Now another is added to the three, and we shall be called the four great masters of the three countries.

CHAPTER VIII

RELEASE AND RETIREMENT, FURTHER CONFIRMATION OF HIS FAITH

EVER since Nichiren was exiled, his followers, especially the warriors connected with the government, had been trying to have him recalled. Nichiren disapproved their plan, and bade them abstain from agitation of that kind. His idea seems to have been that the perils and sufferings heaped upon him were necessary as a means of strengthening the evidence of his mission; it had ever been his conviction that the more faithful the propagator of the Truth was, the stronger would be the opposition and the more severe the persecution. Another reason, as we have seen before, was the idea of expiation; his sufferings, as he conceived it, were all to be endured as the necessary means of expiating the sins accumulated from all eternity by estrangement from the Lotus of Truth.

These subjective reasons for opposing efforts for his release were reinforced by an external consideration. All the steps taken by him up to that moment had for their end the conversion of the government and the nation to his faith. He had done everything he could to bring this about, and finally was sentenced to death. His return to the main island would be useless, unless something new should happen to hasten the accomplishment of his ideals and ends. His release would be acceptable only in case the government authorities should repent of the measures they had taken toward him, and be converted. "I shall never return, until they are willing to yield to my proposals." Judged from several of his own utterances, this seems to have been his determination.[1]

In this frame of mind, Nichiren was watching current events, and looking for the possible repentance of the government. What he especially desired was the fulfilment of his prophecies about approaching dangers from internal disturbances and foreign invasion. And, indeed, events seemed more and more to confirm these predictions. While Nichiren's case was pending, a Mongol ship with one hundred men arrived, causing a panic, although it finally proved not to be a warship. In the following years, 1272 and 1273, Mongol envoys came repeatedly and urged a reply to the messages of the Khan, and the Japanese government was busily engaged in plans for defence, as well as in offering prayers to Shinto and Buddhist deities. Beside the danger from the Mongols, a serious struggle broke out between two Hōjō brothers, which ended in a fratricide. It was after this event that the government, as has been related above, ordered the governor of Sado to give Nichiren a better abode, and to take good care of the exile. Nichiren regarded these occurrences as signs of his success, and at the same time rejoiced in his sufferings as being evidence of his mission. About this time, also, an influential member of the Hōjōs, of the name Tokimori, began to revere Nichiren, and often sent him presents and comforting letters. Although Tokimori seems to have had the superstitious motive of securing Nichiren's intercession with Buddha, and his prayers to avert the threatened invasion, yet he gave progressive evidence of sincere conversion to Nichiren's religion. This was another sign of Nichiren's triumph.

[1] For instance, *Works*, pp. 1414, 1416.

The Hōjōs were not unanimously hostile to Nichiren. Tokimori, the elder, not only showed his good-will toward him, but finally sent a precious sword as a token of the conversion of his Samurai soul to the Lotus of Truth. Nichiren thanked him heartily for it, and advised the convert further to solidify his faith. The letter reads:[1]

I, Nichiren, am perhaps the most intractable man in Japan. I warned you that all manner of disasters would take place, because you worshipped Amita, Dainichi, and those Buddhas whom you held dearer than your parents and more precious than your sovereign; and that you were destined, in this world, to ruin yourselves and cause the fall of the country, and in the future life, to sink to the nethermost hell. Because I gave these warnings incessantly, I am suffering from persecutions . . . I am suffering from the perils heaped upon me by my adversaries, three in kind, simply because I am the one who lives the life of the Lotus of Truth. That you have become a follower of such a man is something beyond common expectation; there must be some significance in the fact. Be strenuous in your faith, and prepare yourself to partake in the communion of the Paradise of Vulture Peak!

You have sent one sword, with its mate, as your offering . . . to the Lotus of Truth. The swords were, while in your hands, weapons of malice; now, being offered to Buddha, they are weapons of good. . . . These swords will serve as staves in your journey beyond. Know that the Lotus of Truth is the staff for all Buddhas on their way to enlightenment! Especially rely on me, Nichiren, as the staff and pillar! . . . The Sacred Title will be your guidance and support on the journey after death. The Buddhas Prabhūta-ratna and Śākya-muni, as well as the four chief Bodhisattvas, will surely lead you by the hand. If I should be there before you, I, also, will not fail to welcome you. . . . I cannot say all I have to say in this letter. Put your faith in all the deities (the guardians of the Truth)! March indefatigably on in the way of faith, and reach your final destiny! Tell your ladies also of all this! Sincerely in reverence.

This letter is indeed significant as evincing Nichiren's affection for a member of the Hōjōs, and as a sign that they were inclining more to him. It is dated the twenty-first of

[1] *Works*, pp. 1032–1034.

the second month (March 30), 1274, just when the sentence of release was on the way to Sado.

Nichiren had in various ways inspired awe in the Hōjōs, and their own troubles caused them to think again of the exile who had spoken like a prophet, and whose predictions seemed to be having their fulfilment. The opinions of the authorities were divided, and Nichiren still had many implacable enemies, but the Commissioner Tokimune finally decided to recall Nichiren to Kamakura. It seems that an intimation of this outcome had been given by Tokimori in the message accompanying the swords. The edict for his release was issued on the fourteenth of the second month (March 23), and reached Sado in the following month, two weeks after the letter above quoted was written, on the eighth of the third month (April 16). Nichiren complied with the order, bade farewell to his followers in the island, and left his abode of two years and a half, as signs of spring were appearing after a long winter, on the thirteenth of the third month (April 21). His religious opponents made attempts on his life at several points on the way, but the guards furnished by the government protected him, and brought him in safety to Kamakura, where he arrived on the twenty-sixth of the third month (May 4), after a journey of two weeks.

It was a triumphal entry for Nichiren. Not only did his old disciples and followers rejoice over the fulfilment of their long-cherished hope, but the government circles seemed to listen to Nichiren, and to seek his advice about the measures to be taken in view of the threatened Mongol invasion. Ten days after the return, on the memorable eighth of the fourth month (May 15), Nichiren was invited to the Commissioner's office. It now became the duty of Hei no Saemon, his bitter enemy, to communicate the good-will of the Commissioner and to make advances to Nichiren. Let Nichiren himself tell the story.[1]

> All of them received me courteously — something quite different from their former attitude. Some asked me questions about Amita-Buddha, others about the Shingon mysteries, others again about Zen. Hei no Saemon himself put questions concerning the efficacy of the teachings current before the revelation of the Lotus. I replied to them all by citing the Scriptures. Hei no Saemon, on behalf of His Excellence, the Commissioner, asked me when the Mongols would come over. I answered that they were to be expected within this year, etc.

Thus the officials showed some readiness to yield to Nichiren's propaganda. He, on his part, did not fail to take the opportunity to renew his strong remonstrances and warnings. His attitude was as aggressive as before, and he showed no disposition to compromise. Nothing would do but that the nation as a whole should at once adopt his religion, while all other religions should be prohibited, and their leaders severely punished. He commented on the many wrongs done by the Hōjō government, not only to himself, but to the religion of Buddha and to the country. Nichiren retired from the palace, and the government was put in a serious dilemma, whether to comply with the demands of the intransigent prophet or to ignore him. Either course seemed to them not only unwise but impracticable. Finally they adopted a compromise, and offered the prophet a great donation, together with high ecclesiastical rank and a public grant for his propaganda. Although the document embodying these proposals which is preserved by the Nichirenites is certainly not authentic, there is little doubt that the authorities wished to see Nichiren's polemics subdued,

[1] *Works*, p. 1406, in a writing containing his reminiscences, written in 1276 — two years after the event, therefore. Similarly, *Works*, p. 1169 (written in 1275); pp. 1241, 1283, 1579.

and to have him join in the prayers for the repulse of the Mongol invaders. Naturally, the prophet would hear to no compromise, but persisted in his demands.

While the question of Nichiren's propaganda was being discussed, the government gave fresh evidence that it had undergone no change of heart, but put its confidence as before in the Shingon mysteries. It was a time of a long drought, and the authorities called on the other Buddhists to pray for rain, as was customary. Nichiren was very indignant. He saw in the offers made to him a deceptive bait, and in the measures taken for rain an open dishonor done to himself. He protested again and again, but the government always vacillated; while his opponents were renewing their accusations and intrigues. The sequel of the triumphal entry was an irreconcilable breach. Nichiren left Kamakura, on the twelfth of the fifth month (June 17), and, taking only a few disciples and retainers, set out for a place among the mountains on the west side of Fuji.

The clamorous prophet was now suddenly changed to a silent recluse or a voluntary exile. Five days' journey brought him to his new abode, and the local chief of the place, Lord Hakiri, one of his warrior followers, welcomed him. A little hut was built in a deep valley in the midst of high peaks, and there the recluse began his new life with a few of his beloved disciples. This place, called Minobu, became Nichiren's home for the last eight years of his life, and, as we shall see later, he regarded it as a paradise on earth because of his residence there.

The change was perhaps quite unexpected, even to his intimate followers, but was a premeditated plan on the part of Nichiren. Various motives have been conjectured for this sudden turn in his life, but he himself, better than any one else, tells us why he made it. The simplest explanation of the matter is given in the words: "I had always resolved to repeat my remonstrance three times, and to retire if these attempts should prove a failure." Now the "three times" is in accordance with an old Chinese proverb, and Nichiren had delivered his message thrice: in 1260, when he had presented his *Risshō Ankoku Ron*; in 1268, when he had repeated the remonstrance as a kind of ultimatum; and now, when he had pressed his demands after the return from Sado. But when we read between the lines, the retirement meant a continuation of his life in exile. It had been his determination not to return to Kamakura, unless the Hōjōs should be completely converted, and now his return had proved a failure. How could he remain peacefully in Kamakura? If he should continue his protests, his fate was plain — another execution or another exile! He was not so blind as to expect anything better. Why should he not become a voluntary exile, instead of a compulsory one? The reception of his third and last remonstrance was the occasion of his retirement, but not its true cause. His motives lay deeper. Let us see what they were.

The first was negative, the idea of expiation. We have already seen that Nichiren conceived his suffering as expiation. His idea was, "Expiation of my sins is the fulfilment of my mission to perpetuate the Lotus of Truth to the coming ages. Sins are not extinguished until the aim be attained." Since his triumphal entry had proved a failure, he must continue the expiation as he had been doing in Sado. Naturally, he associated with expiation a measure of suffering. Whenever he suffered from the extreme cold of Minobu, he must have reminded himself of his first winter in Sado; and he always rejoiced to liken his suffering with the self-castigation of Buddha during his years of self-training among the mountains. "The height of the hermitage is only seven feet, while the depth of snow is ten feet. Ice makes up the walls, and the icicles are like the beads of garlands decorating shrines." [1]

Whenever his followers at a distance sent him food or clothing, he wrote touching letters thanking them for the presents, and likened his benefactors to his parents or to those persons who supplied food to Buddha. His life at Minobu was one of extreme simplicity and austerity, and he never left the obscure spot. The uninviting place, a small piece of level ground, "as large as the palm of a hand," surrounded by high peaks, was his abode for eight years. Here he constructed a hermitage, and rejected Lord Hakiri's offer to erect a larger edifice. It was only in the year before his death that he at last consented to the building of an assembly hall of moderate size; but he enjoyed his abode there as if it were a paradise.

"Expiation" was the thought that constantly occupied his mind, but this idea was, after all, a negative one; the positive, and by far more important, reason of his retirement was his solicitude for the future of his religion. As we have had repeated occasion to note, Nichiren associated every step of his life with some feature of the Scripture, and especially regarded his life in Sado as the chief part, the climax, of his life. Now the last stage was to be inaugurated, and dedicated to the consummation of his mission and to the perpetuation of his religion, just as the last twelve chapters of the Scripture made up the consummation of the Truth. He had proclaimed the Sacred Title at the outset of his ministry; he had furnished the object of worship and spiritual introspection by the graphic representation of the Supreme Being; one thing alone remained — to prepare for,

[1] *Works*, p. 1939 (written in 1280).

or establish, the central seat of his religion. These three instruments of his propaganda were called the "Three Mysteries." Although there are some allusions to them in his writings before this time, Nichiren proclaimed this trinity for the first time in the first essay written after his retirement. This treatise is dated the twenty-fourth of the fifth month (June 24) — just a week after his arrival at Minobu. The great plan which he had long been meditating, and the motive which led him to retire from the present world, and to work for the future, was the establishment of the "*Kaidan*," or the Holy See of the Catholic Church of Buddhism.

In the essay just referred to he says:

> What, then, is that mystery which Nāgārjuna and Vasubandhu, Tendai and Dengyō have not revealed during the more than two thousand years since Buddha's decease? It is nought else but the Supreme Being (*Honzon*), the Holy See (*Kaidan*), and the five characters of the Sacred Title (*Daimoku*), all according to the truth of the primeval Buddhahood. . . .
>
> Behold the tribulations and commotions coming one upon another! They are, indeed, the signs heralding the appearance of the sages, Viśiṣṭa-cāritra and the others. They will appear and establish the Three Gateways to the truth of the primeval Buddhahood. Then, throughout the four heavens and the four quarters will prevail universally the Lotus of the Perfect Truth. Can there by any doubt about this?

[1] The essay is entitled "*Hokke Shuyō-shō*," or "A Treatise on the Quintessence of the Lotus of Truth"; *Works*, pp. 1035–1045.

CHAPTER IX

A PARADISE ON EARTH AND THE HOLY SEE

THE place whither Nichiren retired was surrounded on all sides by high mountains, and when his hermitage was finished in summer time, he doubtless enjoyed cool breezes rustling in the green trees on the slopes. "Like screens," he wrote to a lady in the following winter, "steep peaks surround my abode. On the mountains trees and grasses grow luxuriantly; in the valleys are rolling stones and rocks. Wolves howl and monkeys cry, and the echoes of their voices resound through hill and dale; deer plaintively call the does, and crickets chirp noisily. Flowers that elsewhere bloom in spring, bloom here in summer, and fruits do not ripen till winter. Occasionally human figures are seen, but they are only wood-cutters; or sometimes I have visits from some of my comrades in religion.[1] His mind often turned to retrospection on his past; but what now occupied his quiet thought was rather the future destiny of his religion. As the one foreordained to fulfil the prophecies of the Lotus, he had gone through all perils, and was enjoying the tranquillity of a hermit. A mere secluded life, however, was not his mission. What should he do for the consummation of his life-work, and for the perpetuation of his gospel? This was his question, and he formulated it immediately after his arrival at Minobu. The result was the essay referred to at the close of the last chapter, which was, in fact, intended to be the proclamation of Nichiren's plan, for the accomplisment of which he was about to prepare.

[1] *Works*, p. 1088; dated the sixteenth of the second month (March 14), 1275.

Nichiren's fervor never declined, but in his quiet life as a recluse his mind was occupied, perhaps exclusively, with enthusiasm for his ideal. His method was no longer confined to vehement warnings to the nation, and fiery attacks upon other Buddhists; he reflected calmly, and examined again and again the meaning of the ideal Kingdom of Buddha as the basis of the Buddhist Catholic Church of which his proposed Holy See should be the centre. He was always firm in the conviction that the Holy See was to be established in Japan, the land where the savior of the Latter Days was destined to appear, and where he, the man, was actually born and was doing the savior's work. Yet, on the other hand, his work was not merely for the sake of a small country, composed of many islands. Just as he recognized in his own life two aspects, the actual and mortal, on the one side, and the ideal and eternal, on the other, so he saw in Japan a similar twofold significance, one, the physically limited, and the other, to be realized through transformation according to his high ideal. In this latter sense, Japan meant for him the whole world. He said once: [1]

> The great master Myōraku says in his commentary on the Scripture, "The children benefit the world by propagating the Truth of the Father." "The children" means here the Saints-out-of-earth; "the Father" is the Lord Śākya-muni; "the world," Japan; "benefit" means the attainment of Buddhahood; and "Truth," the Adoration of the Lotus of Truth. Even now, this is not otherwise because "the Father" means Nichiren; "the children," Nichiren's disciples and followers; "the world," Japan; "benefit," the life (of these men) laboring to perpetuate (the Truth) and hasten the attainment of Buddhahood; and "Truth" means the Sacred Title handed down to us from Viśiṣṭa-cāritra.

What he meant was this: Buddhahood, or Truth, is eternal. It can be, and ought to be, made a fact in our own

[1] In the "Dictated Portions of the Lectures on the Scripture"; the lectures given during his retirement and recorded by his disciples.

life. Nichiren is the man sent to lead all to that life, and he is now assisted by his followers, who are, therefore, the Saints prophesied in the Scripture. The attainment of Buddhahood is not a matter of individuals or of the aggregate of individuals, it is the embodiment of the all-embracing communion of all beings in the organic unity of Buddhahood which is inherent in them all. This realization is the Kingdom of Buddha, the establishment of the Land of Treasures, as Nichiren had declared in his *Risshō Ankoku Ron*[1] and explained on many occasions. Now this Kingdom of Buddha is, properly speaking, immanent in the soul of every one, but it can only be realized in the spiritual and moral community of those who are united in the Adoration of the Lotus, and in the worship of the Supreme Being as revealed by Nichiren. This community has been organized by Nichiren, and is growing in the fellowship of his followers. It is to be further extended among their countrymen, and finally to the whole world. The individual, the nation, the world, and the Kingdom of Buddha — these terms stand for different aspects of the one ideal.[2] The Holy Catholic Church of Buddhism is to have the world, the whole cosmos, as its stage; while the cosmos is not to be conceived as a mere universe in space, but essentially exists in the heart of every true Buddhist. Buddha is the Father and Lord of the Kingdom, and his children should strive for the realization of the Kingdom both in their own lives and in the community of all beings.

Nichiren's thinking always aimed, as we have seen, to unite two opposites, and to explain either by reference to the other. This method was applied to the relation between the particular and the universal, between the world and the individual, between human nature and Buddhahood. So

[1] See above, p. 37. [2] For more on this subject, see below, p. 108.

also with the Kingdom of Buddha. It is individual and universal at the same time; either aspect is incomplete apart from the other; individual perfection is inconceivable without the basis of the universal truth, while the universal community cannot exist apart from the spiritual enlightenment of every individual. The Kingdom means the complete working out of the harmonious relation of these two aspects of perfection — Buddhahood. Thus, we see that Nichiren's mind was occupied as much as ever with his own mission and actual life, while at the same time he was thinking no less earnestly on the coming Kingdom of Buddha. He believed himself to be the savior of the coming ages, and was therefore concerned for the future of his religion; but the future was foreshadowed in his present life, and he saw a "Land of Treasures" even in his own hermitage.

"Behold, the kingdom of God is within you!" This was the creed of Nichiren also, witnessed by his life, confirmed by the Scripture, and supported by his metaphysical speculation. When he concentrated his thought on his own calling, he was in communion with the saints in the Lotus; when he expressed anxiety about his country, yet with confidence in its destiny, he was a prophet and an ideal patriot; when he reflected on his tranquil life among the mountains, he was almost a lyric poet, glorifying his surroundings by his religious vision; he was a scholastic philosopher when he interpreted the truths of existence and the nature of the religious community; and he was a mystic in his vision of the future realization of Buddhahood in himself and in the Kingdom of Buddha. Enough has now been said about his conception of his mission, and we shall presently see how he idealized his abode at Minobu; but before taking up this poetic side of his character, let us examine a piece of his scholastic mysticism.

The mystical strain is stronger in the writings from the years of quiet meditation at Minobu than in the preceding period of storm and stress. The best example of this is an essay written in 1279, after four years of retirement. It is entitled, "The Testimony Common to all the Buddhas of the Three Ages."[1] We reproduce the essay in extract.

It is said in the chapter on Tactfulness (chap. II): "According to the model of teaching adopted by all the Buddhas of the three ages, I proclaim the truth which has no distinction (but is universal)."[2] "The truth without distinction" means the perfect truth of the Sole Road. For, in everything, in grasses and trees, in mountains and streams, even in earth and dust, there are present the truths of existence of the ten realms of existence (*hokkai*, or *dharma-dhātu*) which participate in one another; while the Sole Road of the Lotus of the Perfect Truth, which is immanent in our own souls, pervades the paradises in the ten quarters and is everywhere present in its entirety. The fruits (of truth), both proper and subsidiary,[3] are manifest in the excellence and grandeur and beauty of the paradises in the ten quarters. All these fruits are inherent in our own soul, and the soul is in reality identical with the Tathāgata of the primeval enlightenment (in his eternal entity), who is furnished with the three aspects of his personality (the threefold *kāya*). How can there be any other truth besides the soul (in this sense)? One and the same truth pervades the paradises in the ten quarters. This is the Sole Road, and is therefore called "the truth without distinction." . . .

The perfection of truth in the Buddha's soul and the same perfection in our soul are one, and it is inherent in us, and to be realized by ourselves. Thus, there is no truth or existence besides the soul. What we know as our soul (its appearance), its nature (or essence), and its entity (or substance) — these three make up the three aspects of the Tathāgata's personality, (united in) the Tathāgata of the primeval enlightenment.

The Scripture teaches the manifestation (*lakṣaṇa*), the essence (or nature, *sva-rasa*) and the substance (*sva-bhava*) of reality. The Tathāgata of the primeval enlightenment is furnished with these three categories of reality; his body, or substance, is the cosmos, or the realm of truth (*dharma-dhātu*), extending in ten directions; his essence,

[1] In Japanese, *Sanze Sho-Butsu Sōkan-mon; Works*, pp. 1892–1913.

[2] Verse 134; Text, p. 57; SBE., p. 57–58.

[3] This point is explained below; see Appendix.

which is soul, is identical with the cosmos; and his manifestation in glories is manifest in the cosmos also. Therefore our body is one with the body of the Tathāgata, furnished with the three aspects of the primeval enlightenment; it is omnipresent, because it is nothing but a manifestation of the sole Buddha, while all realities represent Buddha's truths.

The paradise means a perfect union of the three aspects, realized in the harmony between the existence and its stage,[1] the existence being the proper fruit, and the stage the subsidiary. . . . The Paradise, or Land of Purity, is the realm of serene light, and is pure, exempt from all depravities; it exists in the soul of every being and is therefore called "The Spiritual Pedestal of the Lotus of the Perfect Truth." . . .

Then the store of truths (Buddha's teachings), eighty-four thousand in the number of its gateways,[2] is nothing but the record and diary of our own life. Everybody rears and embraces this store of truths in his own soul. Illusion occurs when we seek the Buddha, the Truth, and the Paradise outside of our own self. One who has realized this soul is called the Tathāgata. When this state is once attained, (we realize that) the cosmos in ten directions is our own body, our own soul, and our manifestation, because the Tathāgata *is* our own body and soul.

Out of these three fundamental categories of reality spring the following seven, and make up the ten [3] which are the conditions of existence in the ten realms (*dharma-dhātu*). And the ten realms, surging out of the one soul, are revealed in the gateways of truth, eighty-four thousand in number. . . . Thus, the ten categories of existence are united and realized in the origin, and in the consummation. The origin lies in our ultimate being (as defined in the ten terms), and the consummation is embodied in the realization of Buddhahood. The beings are the original (cause and substratum), and the Buddhas are the consummation (result and fruit), because all Buddhas are manifested out of the souls of all beings. And yet the Scripture says:

[1] This is an old Buddhist doctrine. By "Existence" (*bhava*) is meant the nature of being which the individuals within a certain resort of existence manifest, as the result of their common karma, in the qualities of the existence. The "stage" (*dhātu*) means the environs and circumstances of the existence. The former is, therefore, called the "proper fruit" of the common karma, while the latter is the "subsidiary."

[2] The whole extent of Buddha's teachings is said to have 84,000 different aspects. The number is derived from the Tripitaka counted in *ślokas*.

[3] For the ten categories of existence, see the Appendix.

Now the threefold realm of existence is my dominion,
And all beings therein are my children.[1]

. . . This is because Buddha, the awakened, wakes us, who are dreaming the dreams of births and deaths. This awakening wisdom reaches us like the voice of parents calling their dreaming children. Therefore Buddha says that we are his children. Think of this! then Buddha is the Father and we the children, both in the origin and in the consummation, because the fundamental nature and the final destiny are one in the Father and the children. When we perceive, thus, that the soul is one in Buddha and in us, our dreams of births and deaths are broken, and the primeval enlightenment is restored in our awakening. This is the "attainment of Buddhahood in the present life." . . .

When Chuang-Ch'ou[2] dreamt that he became a butterfly, there was none other than Chuang-Ch'ou, just as there was none besides himself when he awoke and knew that he was not a butterfly. When we consider ourselves to be mortals tormented by births and deaths, we are immersed in illusion and delusion, as Chuang became a butterfly in his dream. The original Chuang is restored when we realize that we are the Tathāgatas of the primeval enlightenment; this is the attainment of Buddhahood in the present life. . . . The soul, the Buddha, and existence, these three[3] are laid up in our own soul, beside which there is no reality. This is the enlightenment, Buddhahood. When the truth of the mutual participation between the one and the many, between the particular and the universal, is fully realized, we shall know that everything and all things are found in each existence in the present life. . . . All truths revealed during the lifetime of the Master are only truths existent in ourselves. Know this, and your own entity is revealed. . . .

(All this is fully taught in the Lotus of Truth, and the way to grasp it is to adore the Sacred Title.) Thus maintain harmony with the Buddhas of all times and live the life of the Lotus of Truth! Thereby you will attain the final enlightenment without impediment, and know the relation between self-perfection and the enlightening of others.

This is the testimony common to all Buddhas of the three ages; keep it as a precious mystery!

[1] Chapter iii, verse 87; Text, p. 90; SBE., p. 88.

[2] A Chinese philosopher of the Taoist school, who writes of his metamorphosis into a butterfly, in a dream. Cp. G. F. Moore, *History of Religions*, Vol. 1, pp. 56–58.

[3] The three are the spiritual essence of truths, the personal realization of truths, and the objective manifestation of truths.

Every one who realizes the truth of the fundamental unity is a Buddha, and every one who lives in accordance with this enlightenment and works to propagate the Lotus of Truth is the messenger of the primeval Tathāgata. To such a man, all that surrounds him preaches the truth, and the place of his abode is a paradise. This idea of the connection between the actual life and the primeval enlightenment inspired Nichiren to such a degree that he always regarded his abode as a Buddha-land. He voiced this feeling like a lyric poet, glorifying, thus, the hills and waters of Minobu. In a note [1] (as in several others), he gives utterance to these thoughts:

When the autumn evening draws on, lonesomely, the surroundings of the thatched hermitage are bedewed, and the spiders' webs hanging from the eaves are transformed into garlands of jewels. Noiselessly, deeply-tinged maple leaves come floating on the water that pours from the bamboo pipes, and the water, colored in pattern, seems to stream forth from the fountain of Tatsuta where the Brocade-weaving Lady is said to abide. Behind the hermitage, the steep peaks rear their heads aloft, where on the slopes the trees bear the fruits of "the Unique Truth," and the singing crickets are heard among the branches. In front, flow clear rivulets, making music like drums and flutes, and the pools reflect the moonlight of "reality as it is." When the limitless sky of "entity" is cloudless and the moon shines bright, it seems as if the "darkness of the shrouding delusion" was gone forever.

In the hermitage thus situated, throughout the day we converse, and discuss the truths of the Unique Scripture, while in the evening and late into the night is heard the gentle murmur of the recitation of passages from the sacred text. Thus, we deem that to this place has been transferred Vulture Peak, where Lord Śākya lived.

When fog veils the valley, and even when a gale is blowing, we go to gather wood in the forest, or through the bedewed bushes down to the dells to pick parsley leaves. . . . Reflecting on these conditions of my present life, I often think, so it must have been with Buddha, when he

[1] *Works*, pp. 1297–1306. The title is "*Minobu-san Gosho*," or the "Record of Minobu." It is dated the twenty-five of the eighth month (September 2), 1275.

was in search of truth and disciplining himself in expiation and in mortification.[1] . . .

Thus thinking, I sit on the mat of meditation, and in vision I see every truth present to the mind, so that even the call of a deer to its mate helps me to utter the innermost voice of my heart. Here I realize why, being shrouded by the heavy clouds of illusion, we transmigrate through the nine,[2] while the pure bright moonlight shines within me, the illumination of the threefold aspects of reality [3] fused into one, and the light of the threefold introspection of one and the same soul.[4] Thus, I put my thoughts into verse:

> Masses of clouds and thickening fog,
> Heaping upon me and shrouding the world —
> Let them be dispelled by a freshening breeze,
> The wind that perpetually blows from Vulture Peak,
> Whence streams forth the air of the eternal Truth.

In short, everything in Nichiren's surroundings suggested to him something related to his ideal, and to his present life in service to the Truth. The poet, however, was never content merely to cherish these thoughts, but interpreted his environment by the Scripture. Thus he writes about his abode in the language of the Scripture, and describes his life

[1] There follow several illustrative stories about the former lives of Buddha. All this is summed up in the verse:

> Having served the masters,
> By collecting wood and gathering herbs,
> And by fetching water for them,
> I have at last attained this enlightenment —
> The enlightenment in the Lotus of Truth. . . .

[Indeed, all this is the service of the Lotus of Truth. Similarly, all that Nichiren has done and is doing is for the perpetuation of the Truth, and the salvation of the beings of the Latter Days.]

[2] Nine out of the ten resorts, that is, excepting Buddhahood. The nine are: the Bodhisattava; the Pratyeka-buddha (self-satisfied recluse); the Srāvaka (one content with learning); the Celestial Being; mankind; the Preta (hungry ghost); the Beast, the Asura (furious spirit), and the beings in the hells.

[3] The three are, vacuity, phenomenal appearance, and the view of the Middle Path. See Appendix.

[4] The introspection of the soul under the three categories of reality.

there, as if it were illuminated by the glories of paradise.[1] Not only Minobu, but every place connected with the life of the prophet, of the one who is living the life of the Lotus of Truth, was glorified by him. In a letter[2] written before he left Sado, he says: "I, Nichiren, am a native of Awa, a province of Japan where the Sun-goddess had her abode in the beginning, and founded this nation.[3] . . . She is indeed the loving mother of the people of this country. There must be some remote and mysterious connection with my life, that I, Nichiren, was born in that province." In another letter, written after his retirement in Minobu, he repeats the same idea, and says:[4] "Although Awa is a province far away from the centre, it is somewhat like the centre of Japan, because the Sun-goddess found there her first abode. . . . And I, Nichiren, began the propagation of the true religion by proclaiming it, for the first time, there in Awa."

Sometimes, he speaks more mystically about his spiritual presence everywhere. He wrote from Minobu to a nun in Sado who had served him during his days of exile there, saying in conclusion;[5] "When you long to see Nichiren, look in reverence at the rising sun, or the moon rising in evening. My person is always reflected in the sun and moon. And moreover, hereafter I shall surely meet you in the Paradise of Vulture Peak."

It is by mankind, in all kinds of existence, that the ideal perfection is to be achieved, and therefore the stage of its

[1] A passage of this purport is quoted on p. 108.

[2] Sent to Hōjō Tokimori, dated the twenty-first of the second month (March 30), 1274; *Works*, p. 1034.

[3] This is not found in any legend, but it seems that Nichiren regarded the southeastern corner of Japan as nearest to the place where the sun rises.

[4] Dated the sixteenth of the second month (March 15), 1275; *Works*, p. 1092.

[5] Dated the sixteenth of the sixth month (July 10), 1275; *Works*, p. 1253.

realization is this world, the abode of mankind. The Buddhist ideal of enlightenment is man's awaking to the fundamental unity of his present existence with the primeval Buddhahood; while the key to make this world a hell or to transform it into a heaven is in our own hands. The use of the key consists in first calling forth the primeval Buddahood in the innermost recess of our own soul, and in viewing this actual world as a heaven. This transfiguration means not merely imagining that earth is heaven, but living in conformity with the assumption, under the guidance of the enlightened mind. This ideal was realized by Buddha when he preached the Lotus of Truth on Vulture Peak, and the scene of the revelation was transfigured into a paradise. Nichiren had no doubt about the Scripture narrative, and now, in Minobu, he was himself experiencing such a transfiguration of his own abode. In expressing this conviction, he sometimes spoke, as we have seen, like a lyric poet; yet his poetry was never a mere play of fancy, but an earnest belief, founded on the authority of the Scripture, as well as on his own experience. The union of poetic idealization and religious speculation can be clearly seen in the passages quoted above. Such was Nichiren's thought about the paradise on earth, or rather on the proposition that this very world is paradise [1] to those minds illumined by the truth of the primeval enlightenment.

This conception of the transfiguration of the world is very important for the understanding of Nichiren's idea of the Catholic Buddhist Church, and to make it still clearer we may quote another passage from the dictated portions of his lectures on the Lotus.

[1] In Japanese: "*Shaba soku Jakkō-do,*" that is, the Sahā world itself transfigured into the Realm of Serene Light.

It is said in the Scripture:[1] " At that *time I* shall appear on *Vulture Peak*, *together with* my *congregation*." Here, "time" means the age of the Latter Law, when the spiritual communion (between us and Buddha) shall be realized; " I " means Śākya-muni; " with," the Bodhisattvas; " congregation," the community of Buddha's disciples; "together" implies the ten realms of existence; and "Vulture Peak" is the Land of Serene Light. . . . " Appear " means to make a manifestation at Vulture Peak, while " Vulture Peak " means the manifestation of the Supreme Being, that is, the abode of Nichiren's followers who utter the Adoration of the Lotus of Truth. . . .

Any place where men practise the faith in the Sole Road of Adoration, the adoration of the Lotus of Truth, there is the castle of the eternal Serene Light, which is Vulture Peak. . . . Yet the primeval (entity) of Vulture Peak is nowhere else than in this very Sahā world, especially in Japan, the Land of Sunrise; the Sahā world furnished with the perfection of the primeval stage, where the Lotus of Truth is to be realized; the place where the unique Maṇḍala will be revealed and established — the Maṇḍala embodying the primeval import of what is taught in the chapter on the Life-duration, or the Eternal Life, of the Tathāgata.

Where there lives a true Buddhist, there is manifest in his spirit and life, the Maṇḍala, the cycle embodying the cosmic truth. Where the Truth is manifest, there, is realized the eternal light of Buddhahood, and therefore the place is a paradise. A natural corollary to this idea is that the whole realm of existence ought to be the stage of this realization. But Japan, where the prophet of this gospel has appeared, should be the centre of the Kingdom of Buddha. The man has appeared, and the stage is determined. A definite organization must now be provided for actually effecting the transformation according to the instructions given by the Prophet. This idea gradually crystallized in Nichiren's mind into a definite plan for establishing the centre of the universal church, the Holy See, the *Kaidan*. He had cherished this idea since his days in Sado, and expressed it,

[1] In the sixteenth chapter, Yam., p. 479; Text, p. 324, verse 6; SBE., p. 307.

as we have seen, in the first writing after his retirement. More definite expression was given it in "The Perpetuation of the Three Great Mysteries,"[1] which he wrote on the eighth of the fourth month (April 27), the day believed to be the birthday of Buddha, in 1281. It is also interesting to notice that this year was made memorable by the remarkable prediction Nichiren made to his followers concerning the threatening Mongol invasion. Of this prediction we shall speak later.

The treatise on the Three Mysteries begins with the question, What is meant by the following passage in the chapter (XXI) on the Mysterious Power? "In fine, all the truths possessed by the Tathāgata, all the mysterious powers under the control of the Tathāgata, all the stocks of mysteries cherished by the Tathāgata, all the profound things in the hands of the Tathāgata — all and every one of these have been revealed and proclaimed in this Scripture."[2] This is the famous legacy entrusted to the keeping of Viśiṣṭa-cāritra and other Saints-out-of-Earth. It had been explained in various ways by Nichiren's predecessors, but he interpreted it to mean nothing but the Three Mysteries entrusted to himself, and destined to be fulfilled in the Latter

[1] *Works*, pp. 2051–2054.

[2] Yam., p. 563; Text, p. 391, line 2; SBE., p. 367.

Tendai's commentary bases its famous doctrine of the five "profound principles" on this passage. The five are:

1. The Title . . . The Lotus of the Perfect Truth (*Dharma*).
2. The Entity . . . The mysterious power (*Vṛṣabhitā*).
3. The Principle . . . the stock of mysteries (*rahasyam*).
4. The Efficiency . . . the profound thing (*gambhīra-sthānam*).
5. The Doctrine . . . the revelation and proclamation (*desitam*).

This exegetical development is the basis of Nichiren's idea that the Sacred Title implies all the five principles, and therefore represents the cosmic truth in all its features.

Days, after his time. His interpretation was this: All truths, mysteries, etc., are actuated by the personality of the Tathāgata, while the Tathāgata is a perfect being because he is furnished with the three aspects of personality. The three aspects are: the metaphysical entity (*Dharma-kāya*), which is represented in Nichiren's religion in the Supreme Being, or *Maṇḍala*; the blissful manifestation (*Sambhoga-kāya*), chiefly consisting in intellectual enlightenment, which is represented by the Sacred Title; and the actual manifestation (*Nirmāna-kāya*), the realization of Buddha's mercy, which is to be established and organized in the Holy See, the Sacred Place of Initiation.

Of these three, the first two had already been revealed by Nichiren, and now the foundation of the third was to be laid. He writes about this as follows: [1]

> When, at a certain future time, the union of the state law and the Buddhist Truth shall be established, and the harmony between the two completed, both sovereign and subjects will faithfully adhere to the Great Mysteries. Then the golden age, such as were the ages under the reign of the sage kings of old, will be realized in these days of degeneration and corruption, in the time of the Latter Law. Then the establishment of the Holy See will be completed, by imperial grant and the edict of the Dictator, at a spot comparable in its excellence with the Paradise of Vulture Peak. We have only to wait for the coming of the time. Then the moral law (*kaihō*) will be achieved in the actual life of mankind. The Holy See will then be the seat where all men of the three countries (India, China, and Japan) and the whole Jambu-dvīpa (world) will be initiated into the mysteries of confession and expiation; and even the great deities, Brahmā and Indra, will come down into the sanctuary and participate in the initiation.

Although Nichiren expressed his idea about the time and place of the establishment of the Holy See thus vaguely, he was sure that it would come to pass, and it is related that he despatched the ablest of his disciples to the foot of Fuji to

[1] *Works*, p. 2053.

select the spot for it. Whatever truth there may be in this legend, his conception of the Church and its Holy See was at the same time ideal and concrete. In the ideal, he esteemed every place where his religion should be practised as a paradise; the church embraces all beings, and its stage is the whole cosmos. But, on the other hand, the centre was to be definitely established in a place considered to be peculiarly the source of light and life, in Nichiren's own country. Thus he combined his ideal paradise with the universal church, and spent his days of retirement in silent prayer for the fulfilment of his project. It is no wonder, then, that he pronounced Minobu to be an earthly paradise, and yet planned for the propagation of his religion throughout the world.

CHAPTER X

SILENT PRAYER AND ANXIOUS WATCHING

NICHIREN'S faith in his own mission was firmly established; all the events of his life proved to him the truth of Buddha's prophecies concerning the messenger of the Tathāgata in the Latter Days. In the later years, his thoughts turned more to the future of his religion and his country. His serene delight among the mountains of Minobu was an earnest of the terrestrial paradise that should come in all the world. Probably he offered prayers to Buddha for the fulfilment of this expectation, but he certainly did not lay much weight on any special form of prayer, much less on any ritual such as was employed by the Buddhists of the time. For him, his life in silent retirement was the greatest of prayers, because he believed that the concentrated thought of a true Buddhist ruled the realm of truth, and that by his thought and desire the fulfilment would be hastened.

Though thus living for the future, the present could not be excluded from his mind. In the autumn of the year in which Nichiren retired from the world, the Mongols invaded outlying islands in western Japan, devastated them, and massacred the inhabitants. The invaders, further, succeeded in landing on the larger island of Kyushu, the seat of the government of western Japan, and for a while, occupied that part of the country. The people were in consternation, and the government appealed for help to Shinto and Buddhist deities by dedicating offerings and celebrating mysteries. Nichiren watched the passing events with anxiety, but with a confident faith. His anxiety was of a different nature from the apprehension of the people. He was sure that his country was destined to be a fountain of blessing for the whole world through all coming ages. Yet the government and the people were actually rebels against the true religion of the Lotus, and had not repented as yet of their grave sin in persecuting the prophet, the messenger of Buddha. Therefore, he was no less convinced that Japan was to suffer still greater calamities at the hands of the Mongols. He could welcome the Mongol invaders as instruments of chastisement for the sinful nation, yet he could not harden his heart to the fate of his people in their distress. Righteous indignation and yearning compassion were in conflict within him. He often expressed himself in words like the following: "Behold, now, the danger impending from the fierce Mongols! When they occupy the imperial residence and massacre the people as they did in the western islands, you will undoubtedly ask help of Nichiren. But it will then be too late. Repent, and be converted to the true faith before the hour of the utmost disaster arrives!"

He even went so far as to say that the Mongols were the messengers of Buddha, sent for the chastisement of the unbelievers living in his country. But he did not curse his fellow-countrymen and wish their ruin, nor did he believe that Japan was doomed to such a fate. For example, in a letter addressed to a lady he says: [1]

> You would perhaps rejoice to see my prophetic warning fulfilled, and the Mongols occupying this country. But such a sentiment befits only the common herd (and should not be cherished by my followers). Every faithful follower of the Lotus of Truth should know that he is living in a winter, but also that spring is sure to come after winter.

[1] *Works*, p. 1186; dated the fifth month, 1275.

His thoughts concerning the threatening catastrophe seem to be somewhat conflicting, though his course was clear. He was a fervent patriot, but the country and nation he hoped to see was one completely purged from the sin of rejecting the Truth—the Japanese nation reconstructed and transformed according to his own ideal; while the actual nation was still false to Buddha and his religion. The prospective chastisement of the nation by a foreign invasion was something like a radical cure for a cancer. He saw in the invaders the surgeons, but he never believed that the patient would succumb to the operation. He cursed Japan, but exalted her at the same time, according to these two opposite points of view. This explains the paradoxical character of his expressions in those days of great anxiety. The paradoxes were never, in his own mind, contradictions, but were conceived to be steps toward the fulfilment of his aim.

During this crisis, especially in the year 1275, Nichiren wrote several essays on the future of Japan, explaining also his own attitude toward her perils. The most methodical of them is one entitled "*Sen-ji-Shō*,"[1] the "Selection of the Times." After reviewing the phases of Buddhist history since Buddha's death, he affirms again the conviction he had often expressed before, that his time was the most significant age in the propagation of Buddhism, being the fated fifth five hundred years, in which, as Buddha predicted, a decisive conflict was to take place between the true Buddhism and its opponents. The persecutions heaped upon the prophet, as well as the various calamities that befell the nation, were the signs of the crisis when decision must be made between the truth and falsehood, between the prophet

[1] *Works*, pp. 1189–1250.

and his malignant opponents. To all this Nichiren had borne witness, and now the greatest of the signs, the Mongol peril, heralded the final conflict, to be followed by a miraculous, or rather inevitable, conversion of the whole nation. In other words, the imminent peril was regarded as one of the preparatory steps to the establishment of the Holy See in Japan.

In one passage in this essay he writes: [1]

The Lord Śākya proclaimed to all celestial beings that when, in the fifth five hundred years after his death, all the truths of Buddhism should be shrouded in darkness, the Bodhisattva Viśiṣṭa-cāritra should be commissioned to save the most wicked of men who were degrading the Truth, curing the hopeless lepers by the mysterious medicine of the Adoration of the Lotus of the Perfect Truth. Can this proclamation be a falsehood? . . If this promise be not vain, how can the rulers and the people of Japan remain in safety, who, being plunged in the whirlpool of strife and malice, have rebuked, reviled, struck, and banished the messenger of the Tathāgata and his followers commissioned by Buddha to propagate the Lotus of Truth?

When they hear me say this, people will say that it is a curse; yet, those who propagate the Lotus of Truth are indeed the parents of all men living in Japan. . . . I, Nichiren, am the master and lord of the sovereign, as well as of all the Buddhists of other schools. Notwithstanding this, the rulers and the people treat us thus maliciously. How should the sun and the moon bless them by giving them light? Why should the earth not refuse to let them abide upon it? . . . Therefore, also, the Mongols are coming to chastise them. Even if all the soldiers from the five parts of India were called together, and the mountain of the Iron Wheel (Cakra-vāla) were fortified, how could they succeed in repelling the invasion? It is decreed that all the inhabitants of Japan shall suffer from the invaders. Whether this comes to pass or not will prove whether or not Nichiren is the real propagator of the Lotus of Truth.

Further on he says: [2]

See! Presently, it will not be long before the Great Mongols will send their warships, myriads in number, and attack this country. Then, the sovereign and the whole people will surely abandon all the

[1] *Works*, pp. 1204–1205. [2] *Works*, p. 1240.

Buddhist and Shinto sanctuaries they used to revere, and join in crying *Namu Myōhō-renge-kyō, Namu Myōhō-renge-kyō!* and with folded hands, pray, "O Master Nichiren, save us; O Master Nichiren!"

Then he reviews the history of his persecutions, and the fulfilment of his former predictions, to prove again that to him was given the mission to establish the Buddhist Catholic Church. The conclusion is: [1]

> The greatest of things is the establishment in Japan of this gateway of Truth. How could (the country) be safe, even for a day or an hour, if Śākya-muni, the Lord of the Paradise of Vulture Peak, with the Buddha Prabhūta-ratna, of the realm of Treasure-purity, their manifestations filling the space in the ten quarters, the Saints-out-of-Earth coming from the thousand worlds beneath, and the heavenly beings, such as Brahmā, Indra, the Sun, the Moon, and the four Guardian Kinds, should withdraw (from this country) their protection and assistance, visible and invisible?

All this, especially the last sentence, was a curse indeed. "Cursed be the nation which degrades and offends the Unique Truth!" — this was Nichiren's attitude toward the actual Japan. He rather welcomed the Mongols coming to apply their rude surgery to the deep-seated disease of his nation; yet he had entire confidence in the future destiny of his country, for which, indeed, he himself had a grave responsibility. For he was the messenger of Buddha, commissioned to establish the centre of the world's religion in Japan for the sake of the coming myriad of years. The task of awakening his countrymen rested solely upon his shoulders, and he would fail of his duty if the nation remained unfaithful to the religion. Although he saw in the coming Mongol invasion an agency working for his cause, the final burden of converting the nation was laid upon him. He thus inseparably linked the threatening danger with his

[1] *Works*, pp. 1249–1250.

idea of the future of Japan as well as with his own expiation — the remorseful expiation of his sin of not having thus far accomplished all that he was set to do for the Unique Truth.

The sense of sin lay heavy upon Nichiren's mind, in view of the approaching danger. Japan would certainly suffer from the invaders, as the western islands had been devastated. Was not this because the nation still remained blind to the true Buddhism? Was not he himself chiefly or solely responsible for its blindness? Would not all these perils have been averted, if he had established the Holy See? "All the sufferings that befall my fellow-beings are, after all, my own sufferings."[1] This was his great remorse, caused by the sense of his own sinfulness as well as by concern for his countrymen. His curse was not a product of mere self-righteousness nor of mere hatred of others, but an expression of his deep regret for his country and of his own ideal. There was always, for him, a link between the present danger and the future destiny, between the nation's curse and his own expiation; and this connection was a result of his view of the inseparable tie uniting the individual to the community in which he lives. We have already touched on this point, in discussing Nichiren's ideas about the meaning of the community in human life and in religion.[2] Now, in his grave concern about the threatening invasion, this thought found emphatic expression. A letter which he wrote to a warrior follower, in 1280,[3] is particularly instructive. After dwelling much on the offence committed by the nation against the

[1] *Works*, p. 2038, in the "Warning to the God Hachiman" — to be referred to again below.

[2] See above, p. 98.

[3] *Works*, pp. 1929–1940; dated the twenty-seventh of the first month (February 28), 1280.

Lotus of Truth, he goes on to show how his sufferings were a part of his mission, while he himself cannot but be responsible for the people's folly and their calamities. The individual is never apart from his family and nation; how much more then, must the leader of the nation, the spiritual father of the coming ages, regret and hate his people's folly and suffering! Further, he says: [1]

While Japan is being threatened by the attacks of the Great Mongols, its people are having recourse to the mysteries which are doomed to perish (the Shingon rituals). Are not the ominous records (of their failures) plain in many previous cases? How can a man who knows this remain indifferent to the fact? How sad it is that we have to encounter great calamities, having been born in a country offending and degrading truth and righteousness! Even if we could be personally acquitted of the sin of degrading the truth, how could we be freed from the responsibility for the offence committed by our families and country? If you would be exempt from the offence committed by your family, endeavor to convert your parents and brothers and sisters! The issue will be either that you will be hated by them, or that you will finally convert them all. If you would be free from the offence committed by the country as a whole, make remonstrance to the rulers, and be yourself prepared for death or exile! Is it not said in the Scripture, "Never shrink from sacrificing the body for the sake of the Incomparable Way"? This is explained (by a commentator) as follows: "Insignificant is the bodily life compared with the grave and important cause of the Truth; therefore strive to perpetuate the Truth even at the sacrifice of the body!" That we have, from the remotest past down to the present, not attained Buddhahood, is simply due to our cowardice, in that we have always been afraid of these perils and have not dared to stand up publicly for the Truth. The future will never be otherwise, so long as we remain cowards. All this is deeply impressed upon me by my personal experience.

Even among my followers there are those who dare not to proclaim the Truth, but are content with personal faith alone, and even some who desert the cause, all because they are afraid of the dangers, and care too much for the bodily life, which is, in fact, as evanescent as the dew. Indeed, as is said in the Scripture, "difficult to believe and hard to grasp" is the Truth, and I know by my own experience how diffi-

[1] *Works*, pp. 1937–1938.

cult it is to live the life of the Truth. Traitors are as innumerable as the dust of the earth in all the world, while real believers are as rare as motes on the finger-nails. The offenders are like the waters of the ocean, while the defenders are only but a few drops of water.

Those who remain silent before the opponents of the Lotus of Truth . . . will surely sink to the nethermost hells. Men who, being cognizant of a treasonable plot, do not inform the rulers, are traitors, even if they themselves were not involved in the plot. . . . Remonstrances were made by me, Nichiren, because I knew this truth. A sentence of death, and repeated banishment, were the consequence. Seven years have now passed since I retired among these mountains, wishing to be redeemed from sins, and freed from offences.

To the end of his life, Nichiren never ceased to express these convictions in the strongest terms; but his faith in the destiny of Japan was in no way shaken, nor his self-confidence. On the contrary, the dangers threatening the country and the consternation of the people only strengthened his belief in his great cause and in his own mission. In one of the writings from his years of retirement, he says: [1]

So far as, and so much as, my—Nichiren's—compassion is vast and comprehensive, the Adoration of the Lotus of the Perfect Truth shall prevail beyond the coming ages of ten thousand years, nay, eternally in the future. This is the merit I have achieved, which is destined to open the blind eyes of all beings in Japan (the world), and to shut off the ways to the nethermost Avīci hell. These merits surpass those of Dengyō and Tendai, and are far beyond those of Nāgārjuna and Kāśyapa. Is it not true that one hundred years' training in a heavenly paradise does not compare with one day's work in the earthly world, and that all service done to the Truth during the two thousand years of the ages of the Perfect Law and the Copied Law is inferior to that done in one span of time in the ages of the Latter Law? All these differences are due, not to Nichiren's own wisdom, but to the virtues inherent in the times. Flowers bloom in spring, and fruits are ripe in autumn; it is hot in summer, and cold in winter. Is it not time that makes these differences? Buddha announced, "This Truth shall be

[1] In a letter addressed and dedicated to his old master Dōzen, after his death in 1276. The letter is entitled, "*Ho-on-jō*," or "In Recompense of Indebtedness." (*Works*, pp. 1451–1512; the passage quoted, pp. 1509–1510).

proclaimed and perpetuated in the whole Jambu-dvīpa, in the fifth five hundred years after my death; and it will avail to save all kinds of devils and demons, celestial beings and serpent tribes," etc.[1] If this prediction should not be fulfilled, all other prophecies and assurances will prove false, the Lord Śākya-muni will fall to the Avīci hell, the Buddha Prabhūta-ratna will be burned in the infernal fires, while all other Buddhas in the ten quarters will transfer their abodes to the eight great hells, and all Bodhisattvas will suffer from pains, one hundred and thirty-six in kind. How should all this be possible ? If it is not, the whole of Japan (the world) will surely be converted to the Adoration of the Lotus of the Perfect Truth.

Flowers finally return to the root, and the essence abides in the earth. Let all these merits be dedicated to the soul of the deceased master Dōzen (who had once instructed Nichiren, and is the earth which had nourished Nichiren's wisdom). Adoration be to the Lotus of the Perfect Truth!

This letter illustrates Nichiren's idea that his best attainment should be dedicated to all those to whom he was in any way indebted. But he regarded any such dedication as vain, unless associated with, and practised as a part of, the highest ideal of his religion, the establishment of the Three Great Mysteries. Thus, preceding this conclusion, he reaffirms his own mission to achieve that great task, and expresses his confidence in the approaching fulfilment of his ideal.

Nichiren had a keen sense of thankfulness for benefits of every kind, just as he never excused those who did him wrong. We have seen how he based his ethical theory on the three relations in human life, namely, the relation of a man to his lord, his master, and his parents, and how earnestly he desired to dedicate all his merits to his parents and friends, and even to his persecutors. We have also noted how he spoke of the men and women who supported him in the

[1] This is a quotation from the "*Daishuk-kyō*," or the Mahā-sannipāta (Nanjio, no. 61), which Nichiren often quoted in connection with the Lotus.

worst days of his banishment as if they were reincarnations of his own parents. Similarly, the letters written during his retirement are full of expressions of affectionate gratitude toward those who sent him food or clothing. To a nun who sent him a bag of seaweed, the sight of which màde him homesick for his native place, he wrote:[1]

> When I had nearly forgotten my native place, these seaweeds you kindly sent me awakened in me yearning memories of the familiar scenes of my boyhood. The weeds are like those I used to see in the waters of my native province, the same in color, form, taste, and smell. May it be that they have been sent by my dear parents? I cannot help thinking so, foolish as it may seem.

In short, every one who nourishes him, the man who is living for the sake of the Truth, is father or mother, and is thus contributing to the Buddhist cause. In this way his sense of personal indebtedness was always combined with the consciousness of his high mission; there was nothing in his life that did not present itself in these two aspects — the immediate benefits, and the eternal cause; all practised in the communion of the believers.

The close union of religion and ethics was a characteristic feature in Nichiren's thought and life, and it appears in a harmonious combination of his human sentiments with his religious aspirations. An episode in these years of retirement may serve as an illustration of this union. As has been mentioned in connection with Nichiren's execution, one of his warrior disciples, Shijō Kingo, was always a great favorite of Nichiren. In the sixth month of 1277, Kingo was slandered to his lord by religious opponents. Nichiren wrote to his disciple, admonishing him never to waver in his faith on account of the accusation, and composed for him a defence to be presented to his lord. The lord remained in-

[1] *Works*, pp. 1088–1094; dated the sixteenth of the second month (his birthday), 1274.

flexible, and Kingo was finally deprived of his position and emoluments; yet the faithful warrior not only remained steadfast in his religion, but continued to show admirable fidelity to the lord who had done him injustice. This fidelity made such an impression on his lord that in the following year he restored Kingo to his former position.

All Nichiren's letters about this affair, especially the last ones, expressing his great joy at hearing of Kingo's restoration, exhibit his affection for his disciples, as well as the way in which he counselled and encouraged them. The most touching of these letters is that which was written after Kingo's visit at Minobu, whither he had come to express his gratitude to the spiritual father after the lord had reinstated him. Nichiren had been anxious about Kingo's return journey to Kamakura, fearing that his enemies might attempt his life on the way through mountain-passes. News had now come of his safe arrival, and Nichiren rejoiced at the tidings, but advised continued caution.[1]

When you left me here to go back, my soul almost died in me; and now I hear of your return to Kamakura without any danger. What a joy and relief it is to me! I was so anxious about you that I asked everybody that came from along your route. My anxiety was relieved, step by step, when I was told that you had been seen at Yumoto, then at Kōzu, and at last at Kamakura. Hereafter, you must not come over here, unless on urgent business. If you have anything to consult me about, send a messenger! Indeed, your coming here the last time caused me too much anxiety; think of my concern about you!

Commonly, your enemies have their eye on you when you are beginning to forget them. If you should hereafter go on a journey, never leave your horse behind you! Select your retainers and furnish them with armor! You yourself must go on horseback.

It is said, "The protection of the gods is given to those who are strong and prepared." The Lotus of Truth is a sharp sword, but its effectiveness rests with the one who uses it. . . . Therefore, be strong

[1] *Works*, pp. 1817–1820; dated the twenty-second of the intercalary tenth month (December 7), 1278.

and discipline your mind! . . . If your faith in the Lotus of Truth be firm and strong, all perils will vanish before it. Thus thinking, be steadfast in your faith!

One month before this visit, when Nichiren was informed of Kingo's restoration, he wrote him a letter of encouragement, which well shows how human sentiment and religious aspiration were connected in Nichiren's mind.[1]

> He who endures constant persecutions, in the beginning, in the middle, and to the end, is the messenger of the Tathāgata. I, Nichiren, am not quite the messenger of the Tathāgata, for I am a common man. Yet something like the messenger am I, who have twice been exiled on account of the hatred of the three classes of my opponents. I am something like the messenger, because my mouth utters the Sacred Title of the Lotus, although, for my person, I am just a common mortal, inflamed by the three kinds of passions.[2] To seek a parallel in the past, I am like the Bodhisattva Sadāparibhūta; and in my present life are being fulfilled the prophecies about the one who should suffer from sticks, and swords, and stones. Can I, then, entertain any doubt about the fulfilment of the promise of being taken to the Holy Place? How, then, shall not those who are nourishing me (like you) enjoy the communion of the Land of Purity?

Thus, all those who live in communion, united by the Adoration of the Lotus of Truth, are fellows of the universal and eternal fraternity. Within the communion, however, there are relations of parents and children, of master and disciples — the aspects of human life which remain through eternity, as in the case of the primeval Buddha and his disciples, and similarly in that of the prophet and his followers. Yet this relation does not mean mere subordination on the part of the disciples, but gratitude, and its fruit, the perpetuation of the truth transmitted and committed to them. This idea has already come out in the relations

[1] *Works*, p. 1792; dated the fifteenth of the ninth month (October 6), 1278.

[2] Greed, hatred, and stupidity.

between Buddha and other beings, when we were considering Nichiren's conception of the Supreme Being.[1] Applied to the fellowship of believers in the Buddhist Church, the same kind of reciprocity of benefaction and gratitude, of entrusting and perpetuation, exists between Nichiren and his followers forever. Consequently, the Church is the organ for perpetuating Nichiren's ideals through the efforts of his followers. Seen in this light, every quickening and inspiring legacy of thought left to his disciples was Nichiren's preparation for the future establishment of the Holy See; and he believed that the approaching Mongol invasion would hasten the realization of his ideal, which was to come about through the repentance and conversion of the Japanese people.

Nichiren's great aim was to achieve his ideal of the Catholic Church, with its centre in his own country. Believing that he was himself the man to do this, and that the true import and end of Buddhism had not been apprehended in earlier times, even in India, he saw in vision a return of Buddhism from Japan to India, and its propagation thence throughout the world. He himself was always the cardinal factor in this new era, but the time and place were essential conditions of the realization of this universal Buddhism. Thus, he writes:[2]

That India was called the country of the Moon-tribe[3] was prophetic of the appearance of Buddha (in that country). Our Fusō[4] is

[1] See above, p. 79.

[2] In a treatise entitled, "*Kangyō Hachiman Shō*," or "Warnings given to the God Eight Banners"; written in 1280. *Works*, 2021–2041; quotation from p. 2040.

[3] That is, the Yuechis. The idea that India was the country of the Moon-tribe was combined with another tradition identifying the name India with Indu, the moon.

[4] The name of a certain kind of tree called *fusō* was sometimes employed by the Chinese as an appellation of Japan.

called Japan, the Land of Sunrise. Must it not be the country where the (predestined) Sage should appear ? The transit of the moon shifts from west to east; this symbolizes the transmission of the Buddha's religion to the East. The sun rises in the east and sets in the west; this is an omen that the Buddhist religion shall return from the Land of Sunrise to the country of the Moon-tribe. The moon is not bright all the time, and just so (Buddha proclaimed the Perfect Truth) only during eight years of his life.[1] The sun surpasses the moon in brilliancy, and in like manner (the light of the eastern Sage) is destined to illumine the dark ages after the fifth five hundred years.

While Nichiren's thought was soaring on in such visions of the coming Church, the Mongol menace also engaged his mind. The "Warning to the God Hachiman," above cited, was indeed meant to be an emphatic monition—now, not to the prejudiced people, but to the god who was believed to be the guardian of the country, and an embodiment of the nation's militant virtues. Indeed, while the "Warning" was in hand,[2] the Mongols were busily engaged in preparations for sending their "Invincible Armada," as the last attempt upon the island nation. When, in the year following (1281), the prophet committed to writing the "Three Great Mysteries," as his spiritual legacy, the armada had already left the shores of China and were swarming along the Korean coasts. One month later (in the fifth month, June), four thousand warships appeared on Japanese waters, and came to anchor in the bay of Hakata, in western Japan. The excitement was great, and undoubtedly the news reached the prophet's hermitage. The circular sent by him to his followers is very characteristic.[3]

[1] Buddhist tradition puts the preaching of the Lotus of Truth in the last eight years of Buddha's ministry.

[2] It is dated the twelfth month, and therefore was written either in December of 1280 or in January of 1281.

[3] "The Circular about the Little Mongols"; *Works*, p. 2055.

Now the *Little Mongols* have come to attack *Great Japan*. All my disciples and followers should keep silence, and not discuss the matter either with others, or among themselves. Any one who violates this command shall be excommunicated. Let this be made known to all.

The circular is dated the sixteenth of the sixth month (July 3), 1281, when the defenders on the western coasts were struggling against the arrows and bombs of the Mongols. The expression is so terse that it can be taken in more than one way, especially when we remember that Nichiren had always seemed to hail the Mongols as an instrument to awaken the nation. But one thing is clear; in this letter he used for the first time the phrase, "the *Little* Mongols," the opposite of the usual designation, the "*Great* Mongols." The Mongols, physically great and formidable, were little from the prophet's point of view; while, as is evident from his previous writings, the actual Japan was for him a degenerate nation, doomed to ruin, but the ideal Japan was great and impregnable.

It was on the first of the intercalary seventh month (August 15) of 1281 that a storm destroyed the Mongol armada, which had not effected a landing, and thus the invasion proved a total failure. On the very day when the Mongol warships were being shattered by the hurricane, Nichiren wrote to a warrior disciple, who was probably setting out to join the defenders, saying:[1]

When the Mongols sent their ultimatum, coming on top of the previous calamities of earthquakes, etc., I gave warning to the authorities, but they did not give heed. Now, Nichiren's predictions are being fulfilled, and the battle is raging. All the people of the country will certainly become in this present life *Asuras* (furious spirits), and fall hereafter to the nethermost hells. You may die in the battle. . . . Yet be sure that we shall meet in the Paradise of Vulture Peak! Even if you should share in the calamity, your soul is in communion with

[1] *Works*, p. 2061.

Buddha's soul. In this life you are participating in the life of the "furious spirits," and yet you will surely be born in Buddha's land after death.

All other letters written during a few months after the great event are full of this sentiment. The prophet seems not to attach much importance to the "great victory" won by the help of a storm, which was believed by the people to have been sent by divine intervention. In one of these letters he says: [1]

> An autumn gale destroyed the enemy's ships, and now the people boast of a great success, as if the commander of the enemy had been captured; while the priests pretend that it was due to the efficacy of their mysteries. Ask them whether they took the head of the Mongol king? Whatever they may say, make no other reply than this!

In reality, the defeat of the invaders was of momentous consequence; most of the soldiers were drowned, though the story that only three men escaped must be an exaggeration. The people rejoiced, and the priests gloried in their achievements in prayer; but Nichiren looked at the event with a cool aloofness, probably thinking how remote the fulfilment of his ideal was. He still insisted that the nation could not really be saved, except by complete conversion.

Nichiren may have been mistaken, if he thought that the success of an invasion by the Mongols would prove the truth of his predictions; but he was certainly right in not being elated by the victory. He was far-sighted enough to recognize that the curse that rested on the nation was a long way from being removed by the defeat of the Mongols. Historians know today that the evils of the superstitious mysteries against which Nichiren fulminated increased in consequence of the unexpected end of the Mongol armada,

[1] Sent to Lord Toki, the old warrior, and dated the twenty-second of the tenth month (December 4) of 1281.

because the authorities were themselves too superstitious to resist the exorbitant demands made by the Shinto and Buddhist priests and sorcerers for further contributions toward the support of mysteries and supplications, on which much wealth was lavished. Priests were prized more highly for their prayers than the fighters who had prevented the Mongols from landing and kept them for three months on the sea, until the storm came. Measures for defence against future attacks, were concerted; but unwisely, from the strategic point of view, these measures were confined to the land, little attention being paid to the navy. Yet a worse thing was the extravagant outlay in building and decorating the temples and shrines of those deities who were believed to have rescued the country; the expenditure on them being estimated to have been much more than for any other purpose. Discontent was growing among the warriors, financial difficulties became more and more serious, and the final result was the collapse of the Hōjō government in 1333, which was followed by social disintegration. The defence was successful only by chance. Subsequent events proved that that "miraculous" relief was largely responsible for the age of war which lasted three hundred years after the fall of the Hōjōs.

Whatever might have been the effect of the victory on Nichiren's mind, it is interesting to notice that one of his letters written not long after the event (dated the eleventh day of the ninth month — October 22), takes a high flight, and may be regarded as the crowning expression of his ideas about himself and the transfiguration of this world.[1]

[1] *Works*, pp. 2069–2070. There are many other passages dealing with the coming transformation of this world. It was his belief that the conversion of the whole world would result in the transformation of the earthly realm into a paradise. Cp. *Works*, pp. 391, 402, 476, 1052, 2051, 2078, etc.

This spot among the mountains is secluded from the worldly life, and there is no human habitation in the neighborhood—east, west, north, or south. I am now living in such a lonely hermitage; but in my bosom, in Nichiren's fleshly body, is secretly deposited the great mystery which the Lord Śākya-muni revealed on Vulture Peak, and has entrusted to me. Therefore I know that my breast is the place where all Buddhas are immersed in contemplation; that they turn the Wheel of Truth upon my tongue; that my throat is giving birth to them; and that they are attaining the Supreme Enlightenment in my mouth. This place is the abode of such a man, who is mysteriously realizing the Lotus of Truth in his life; surely such a place is no less dignified than the Paradise of Vulture Peak. As the Truth is noble, so is the man who embodies it; as the man is noble, so is the place where he resides. We read in the chapter on the "Mysterious Power of the Tathāgata" as follows:[1]

"Be it in a forest, or at the foot of a tree, or in a monastery, . . . on that spot erect a *stupa* dedicated to the Tathāgata. For such a spot is to be regarded as the place where all Tathāgatas have arrived at the Supreme Perfect Enlightenment; on that spot all Tathāgatas have turned the Wheel of Truth; on that spot all Tathāgatas have entered the Great Decease." Lo, whoever comes to this place will be purged of all sins and depravities which he has accumulated from eternity, and all his evil deeds will at once be transformed into merits and virtues.

[1] The twenty-first chapter, Yam., p. 564; Text, p. 391; SBE., p. 367.

CHAPTER XI

THE LAST STAGE OF NICHIREN'S LIFE AND HIS DEATH

THE prophet had nearly reached the sixty-first year of his age, and for some time his health had been impaired. " Since I retired to this place, I have never been out of these mountains. During these eight years, illness and age have brought me severe suffering, and both body and mind seem to be crumbling into ruin. Especially since last spring, my illness has progressed, and from autumn to winter my weakness has increased day by day. During these ten days, I have taken no food, and my suffering is aggravated by the severe cold in the midst of a huge snowfall. My body is like a piece of stone, and my chest is as cold as ice." [1] The words are from a letter to a lady who had sent him rice and rice-beer, thanking her for the comfort her drink had brought him. Even a strong man of almost superhuman will, like Nichiren, was unable to resist the disease, which was doubtless the result of constant strife and suffering through thirty years of his life. His mind was perhaps preoccupied by his illness, and we have only eleven letters from the ten months preceding his death; yet some of these letters are still in a vigorous strain, and he dwells much on the ideals of his mission, in contrast to the actual condition of the country. He was a prophet to the last moment.

A letter that he wrote to Lord Toki is interesting as embodying Nichiren's thoughts on disease. Toki had written

[1] Dated the eighth of the twelfth month of the fourth year of Kōan (January 19, 1282). *Works*, p. 2082. These statements indicate that his illness was a cancer of the digestive organs.

to the Master about a plague that was raging in the country, and, it seems, had asked his opinion. In reply, Nichiren explained that there were two causes of the plague, one bodily and the other mental, which were reciprocally related, and produced by the malicious devils, who seize every opportunity of attack. The devils are, however, Nichiren says, nothing but the radical vices existing in each one of us from eternity; because both goods and ills are, according to Tendai's conception of existence, inherent in our own nature. Not only diseases, but *all* evils are only manifestations of the radical and innate vices, and there will be no cure until these vices have been extirpated. Then the question is, Why are the faithful believers of the Lotus of Truth attacked by ills or devils? For the solution of this problem Nichiren has recourse to the doctrine of "mutual participation." Just as the bliss of enlightenment in a particular individual is imperfect unless this bliss is shared by all fellow-beings, so ills may attack even the holders of the Truth, even the messenger of the Tathāgata, so long as there exists any vice in the world in any of his fellow-beings. And the believers of the Lotus are perhaps more frequently attacked by ills, because the devils, regarding the *true* Buddhists as their most formidable adversaries, aim particularly at their lives.

Such was Nichiren's thought on illness in general. Applied to his own person, it was associated with his mission to establish the Holy See. So long as the true Buddhism was taught only in theory, as was done by Tendai and Dengyō, the onset of the devils was not so violent as when the theory was translated into practice, as it was by Nichiren. This was the reason why he encountered so many perils as a result of his aggressive propaganda; they were to be explained in the same way as the illnesses which attacked him and his followers. In other words, the radical vices, and consequent ills, were aroused to rage by Nichiren's propaganda, especially by his preparations for the establishment of the Holy See. When this latter end should be completely achieved, there would be no more room for the vices to have their evil way. Seeing this, the devils run riot, for the purpose of staying the progress of the cause. Thus, Nichiren saw in the raging plague, and also in his own illness, a sign of the approaching fulfilment of his aim. "Does not the growing stubbornness of the resistance show the strength of the subjugating power? Why, then, should not the true Buddhist suffer, not only from illness but from perils of all sorts? Is not Nichiren's life itself a living testimony to this truth?" Thus he wrote in a letter dated the twenty-sixth day of the sixth month, "1282,"[1] which he meant to be his own sermon on illness and death, corresponding to Buddha's sermon in the Book of the Great Decease.[2]

"Our Lord Buddha revealed the Lotus of Truth on Vulture Peak, during eight years, in the last phase of his earthly life; then he left the Peak, and went northeastward to Kuśināgara, where he delivered the last sermon on the Great Decease, and manifested death." This tradition occupied

[1] Further study has led the author to the conclusion that this letter really belongs in the year 1278, that is, four years earlier than it is dated by the editor of the *Works*. In that year pestilence was raging, and Nichiren was suffering greatly, too, from the illness which finally proved fatal. The statement is left as it was first written, before this conclusion was arrived at, because the difference of date does not in any way affect the significance of what is said in the letter.

[2] The *Mahā-Parinirvāṇa-sūtra*, a Mahāyāna counterpart of the Pali *Mahā-Parinibbāna*, for which see SBE, vol. xi. The Mahāyāna book on Buddha's death was believed by Nichiren to have been preached subsequently to the revelation of the Lotus.

Nichiren's ideas about the radical vices are derived from Buddha's attitude toward Māra. See Windisch, *Buddha and Māra*.

the mind of Nichiren, who had lived a life of sixty years in thorough-going conformity to, or emulation of, Buddha's deeds and work. On the eighth of the ninth month (October 10), he left his beloved retreat at Minobu, where he had lived for more than eight years. His intention had been to go to a hot spring, but, probably because he was unable to proceed farther, he stopped at Ikegami, near the modern Tokyo, where he was welcomed by Lord Ikegami. The letter he wrote on his arrival at Ikegami, to Lord Hakiri in Minobu, was his last. This letter, dated the nineteenth (October 21), is full of delicate sentiment, and in it he again expresses his thanks for the protection extended to him by Lord Hakiri during more than eight years. He even gives thought to such details as the care of the horse which, with its harness, Lord Hakiri had presented him. Thenceforward, he lay on a sickbed. During nearly a month he lectured again on his old *Risshō Ankoku Ron*, with which he had launched upon his career of conflict and danger. The lectures were unfortunately not recorded, but we can imagine how the prophet reviewed and reinterpreted the most significant document of his whole life in the light thrown on it by his experiences through more than twenty years.

His disciples and followers flocked to his bedside, and the master charged them with the work to be done after his death. Six elders were appointed to be the leaders, and they took a vow to perpetuate the legacy of the master. Besides them, an important appointment was made, of a boy[1] of fourteen to whom was committed the task of converting the Imperial family in Miyako. The motive of the selection is not clear, but whatever it may have been, the boy subsequently proved himself deserving of the Master's confidence,

[1] He was named Nichizō, concerning whom see the Chronological Table at the end of the book.

and became the pioneer of the propaganda in the Imperial capital.

When all had been finished, Nichiren's last hour approached. Early in the morning of the thirteenth day of the tenth month (November 14), 1282, surrounded by his devout followers, and reciting with them the Stanzas of Eternity, the prophet passed away. The stanzas are: [1]

Since I attained Buddhahood,
Aeons have passed, the number of which
Is beyond all measure, hundreds and thousands
Of millions of billions, and immeasurable.

During this time I have constantly been preaching truths,
And leading innumerable beings to maturity,
Taking them on the Way of the Buddhas;
Thus, innumerable aeons have passed, ever in the same way.

For the sake of awakening all beings,
I manifest the Great Decease, by the method of tactfulness;
And yet in reality I never vanish,
But reveal truths by being eternally present. . . .

I am the Father of the world,
The One who cures all ills and averts disasters.
Since I see the mass of men infatuated,
I appear to die, although I am really living.

For, if they saw me perpetually abiding among them,
They might grow slack,
Become careless, and being attached to the five passions,
Finally fall into the woeful resorts.

I am ever watching to see whether all beings
Are faithful to the Way or not;
And I preach to them various aspects of truth,
According to their capacities, and for the sake of their salvation.

Thus, my constant solicitude is,
How can all beings
Be led to the incomparable Way,
And ere long attain Buddhahood?

[1] Cp. Text, pp. 323 f.; SBE., vol. xxi, pp. 307 f.

APPENDIX

APPENDIX

THE BUDDHIST CONCEPTION OF REALITY

I. The Fundamental Tenets of Buddhism concerning Reality

BUDDHISM is a comprehensive system of thought. In it we find a materialistic school, which denied the existence of the mind and affirmed the reality of the external world; there was also an extreme idealistic school, which explained all perceptions and phenomena as illusions. Moreover, in Buddhist thought, philosophical theories are intricately interwoven with religious faith regarding the person of the founder; and, similarly, the various ways of practising contemplation are inseparable from ethical considerations which bear upon the religious, or ecclesiastical, community. The mind is minutely analyzed; yet Buddhist psychology was not a theoretical study, but was considered to be a means of introspection in meditation, which in turn very much influenced the psychological theories in question. The law of causation was the chief tenet of Buddhist cosmology; but for Buddhism this conception was highly teleological, being understood in the sense of moral retribution. Morality is taught, of course; and every Buddhist is expected to observe its rules; the moral ideal, however, was not limited to human life, but extended to all kinds of existence, visible and invisible. A religious ethic, or a philosophical religion, or a religious philosophy — each one of these designations may be applied to Buddhism; while in the numerous schools within it different points have been given prominence.

Thus, to abstract a phase of Buddhist thought, apart from other factors, is as if one were to dissect a human body into parts, and treat one of them as a unit. As a Buddhist simile expresses it, none of the numerous diamonds studded on a net can be touched without affecting all the others. Yet I shall try here to take up one aspect of Buddhist thought concerning reality. It would be an altogether hopeless task, if there were not a certain continuity of thread even in the meshes of a net. And this continuity is given in the conception of Dhammā, which means "law," or "truth." This is one of the Buddhist Trinity, the others being Buddha and Sangha, that is, the person of the founder and the community of believers. This Trinity is the foundation of the Buddhist religion, and none of the three is perfect apart from the others. It will presently appear how the Buddhist conception expressed in the idea of Dhammā is supported by, and connected with, the faith in Buddha, the revealer of truth. But I shall start with the idea of Dhammā, apart from the other terms of the Trinity.

Dhammā (in Sanskrit, *Dharma*) is a very flexible term in Buddhist terminology. It meant originally, in the Brahmanic idea, "what endures," that is the law of social order. Buddha adopted this term, divorced from its association with social sanction, and used it to designate his teachings about the truths of existence. These teachings were expressed in words and preserved in writings, although to the Buddhist they were not merely letters or words, but truths, and therefore things, as well. Buddha is the revealer of truths as they are in reality, and the doctrines are proclaimed in accordance with the reality of things. That is the reason why the word Dhammā, especially when used in the plural, means things, or conditions, or realities, both mental and physical. These things and conditions are not products of chance, but exist and change according to the definite order of laws, or truths. This order of truth is expressed pre-eminently by the law of causation, which is assumed by Buddhism to be universal and irrevocable throughout all changes of the world. "That being present, this comes to be; because that has arisen, this arises" — this is the key-note of the Buddhist view of the world. The law of causation is applied to the physical and mental orders of existence, to the subjective and objective aspects of our being. It is the essential nature of things and processes that they are through and through ruled by the same Dhammā of causation.

Partly because of the assumption of universal causality, and partly because of its religious ideal of communion, Buddhism assumes the basic unity of existence, notwithstanding the fact that it admits apparent diversity. We comprehend the Dhammā of the external existence, because the same Dhammā is inherent in us; we understand other people, because they are beings subsisting by the same Dhammā. Thus, the fundamental nature of all Dhammās is one and the same. The fundamental nature of existence (*dhammā*), in this sense of unity, is called *dhammatā*, that is, the essential quality of being subject to the laws of existence. Dhammās exist and become such as they are (*yathābhūtam*), and yet they are one in nature and in relation. Everything that is born and grows is subject to age, ills, and death — this is the essential nature of things. All Buddhas, of the past, present, and future, have attained, and will attain, the highest freedom by treading the same way of perfection — this is the universal qualification (*dhammatā*) of Buddhas. Buddha's teachings and injunctions aim at the purification of the mind, and are efficacious to lead us up to the supreme enlightenment — this is the invariable import of the Dhammā. The term Dhammatā applies to every one of these aspects of the universal nature. The same idea is expressed adverbially by the word *tathatayā*, that is, in accordance with nature, and as a noun by *tathatā*, i. e., "as it is," or "*Thatness.*" Therefore, Buddha is called Tathāgata, the One who has attained the Truth of existence, the Dhammatā or Tathatā of the world, and has come to reveal the same truth to us. He is the Truth-winner and Truth-revealer. Because the Dhammatā is the same in him and us, his truth is revealed to us, and *we* are enlightened by the same truth.

The Dhammā is the truth revealed by Buddha, the Lord of Truth; yet he is not the creator of it. We are enlightened by the truths taught by him, but we can be thus enlightened because our existence and nature are based on the same Dhammatā that is found in Buddha himself. The final Dhammatā is the fountain of Buddhist attainment and revelation, for Buddha as well as for ourselves. The world of Dhammās is a perpetually flowing stream; foam and flakes float on its surface, but one can attain the tranquil ocean of Nirvāna by pursuing the course of the stream; after all, one and the same is the water in the fountain, in the stream, and in the ocean. Seen in this way, the fundamental Dhammatā of things and beings is the source of illusion as well as of enlightenment, of vices as well as of virtues. One who does not realize this unity is in illusion, while one who has grasped the Dhammatā or Tathatā, is a Buddha. It is said:

> All are subject to the laws (*dhammās*) of ill,
> Of age, as well as of death;
> Beings exist according to the laws.
> (*yathā dhammā, tathā sttā*). (*Anguttara*, v. 57.)

The deluded are distressed by these changes, while the enlightened man is not troubled by them because he knows the truth. The Truth is permanent, even independent of persons who are troubled by it, or are enlightened in it. Again, it is said:

> Where there is birth, age and death necessarily follow. This realm (of causal nexus) is perpetual, regardless of the Tathāgata's appearing or not appearing (in this world); and the stability of truth (*dhammā-tthiti*) and the order of truth (*dhammā-niyāmatā*) follow their necessary and natural concatenation. The Tathāgata has comprehended this, and penetrated into the Truth; having comprehended and penetrated into it, he announces and preaches it, makes it known, establishes and reveals it, and makes it clear and visible.
> (*Samyutta*, 12. 20.)

Herein is a point of great importance, which gave rise to two opposite interpretations of Buddha's teachings. One school understood in this thesis the permanent stability of the Dhammā, meaning thereby external existence; while the other interpreted the stability of truth as existing in our own mind. The difference may be stated thus: The school which emphasized the objective import of the Dhammā ran to an extreme verging on materialism, asserting the reality of the external order, and denying the mind, on the ground of the doctrine of *non-ego*. The opposite direction was taken by the other school, which saw no meaning in what is usually spoken of as the objective world, apart from its significance as a manifestation of the universal Dhammatā. The consequence was that the truth of existence was to be realized only in the enlightened mind of a Buddha, and that, therefore, reality belonged, not to the world of visible diversity, but to the realm of transcendental unity. The former tendency was represented by the Sarvāsti-vādins, the men who asserted that "all exists"; who were opposed by nearly all others, though the extreme transcendental view was not universally accepted. Before taking up the opposition, we must inquire what Buddha's own position was.

Buddha always explicitly repudiated the two extremes, the Permanence-view (*Sassata-vāda*) and the Nihilistic view (*Uccheda-vāda*), that is, the views which either assert or deny the reality of the external world *per se*. He once said to his great disciple, Kaccāna:

> The world, for the most part, holds either to a belief in being (*atthi*) or to a belief in non-being (*natthitam*). But for one who, in the light of the perfect insight, considers how the world arises, belief in the non-being of the world passes away. And for one who, in the light of the perfect insight, considers how the world ceases, belief in the being of the world passes away. . . . That all is existent (*sabbam atthi*) is one extreme; that all is non-existent (*sabbam natthi*) is another extreme. The Tathāgata, avoiding the two extremes, preaches his truth, which is the Middle Path.
>
> (*Samyutta*, 12. 15; Warren, p. 165.)

The former view is that of common-sense realism, which Buddha refuted by showing how change and decay actually go on before our eyes. Buddha opposed this kind of realism, not by denying reality altogether, but by demanding a change in the conception of reality, a transfer of the idea of reality from the conception of permanent external existence to that of becoming ruled by the law of causation. On the other hand, the nihilistic theory differs from Buddha's position in a very subtle manner, because Buddha rejects the idea of permanence, yet sees reality in things and processes; both being Dhammās by virtue of the same law. He accepts the assertion that nothing exists in the sense that nothing persists by itself; but he rejects the same assertion by making a counter-affirmation that reality consists in the stability and order of truth, of the law of causation. This is what he called the Middle Path, as he preached the Middle Path in his ethics, rejecting both the hedonistic life and ascetic self-mortification.

The Buddhist realism above referred to was in fact not so materialistic as it was believed to be by the opposing schools. Yet it concentrated its effort upon an analysis of the Dhammās, as if they were merely external existences, and neglected the significance of Buddha's Tathāgataship, which consisted in his having grasped the truth of existence in his enlightened mind. The realists missed the point in their conception of Dhammā, because they proceeded to its analysis, apart from the ideal interpretation of the Dhammās as given by Buddha himself. Thus, this school of realists was controverted by adducing the personal example of Buddha, and by emphasizing the significance of faith in him as the Tathāgata, in the conception and interpretation of reality. In other words, the opposition took the orthodox course of never separating the conception of Dhammā from the personality of Buddha as the Truth-winner and Truth-revealer.

Now, not speaking of the extreme transcendentalism, the orthodox theory of the Middle Path may be formulated in the following way:

Buddha has unquestionably said that the truth-order exists and works, regardless of whether a Tathāgata appears, or not. But, who among Buddhists could, without his revelation of Dhammā, have realized that truth? In fact, the external-realist asserts the truth-order in consequence of Buddha's teaching; and Buddha taught this because the truth was grasped by him. This we say, not merely in the sense that Buddha is our authority in this matter, but in the sense that the truth-order would remain a meaningless entity or process, unless there were at least one man who had realized it and interpreted its meaning. Undoubtedly, the truth-order may be working, even while you or I do not realize it. Yet it has become known to us through Buddha's revelation, and then in our own enlightenment. Enlightenment and revelation are the essential factors in the nature of the truth-order, because the conception truth-order does not mean a dead entity, nor a merely external order, but implies a realization of its import in the enlightened mind, which represents the ideal order of existence.

Otherwise expressed, the world, the realm of truths (*dhammā-dhātu*), as a whole, is the stage on which the beings in the world attain their own Dhammatā; and therefore the world, subsisting by itself, but without knowing its own meaning—its own truth-order—is an imperfect manifestation of its real nature. Only a half, and the inferior half, of reality, of the real nature of existence, is rightly to be conceived as the merely external existence; the other half, the essential and integral half, is first revealed to us when we bring to light our own real nature. It is a realization of the Dhammatā, on my part or yours; this is, however, not a merely individual work, but the enlightenment of an individual mind as a part of the world, nay, as the key to the revelation and realization of its real nature. Reality (Sanskrit, *dharma-tathatā*, *dharma-svabhava*) is nothing but a full realization of the true nature; and in the true nature of the world, the ideal interpretation plays no less part than what is erroneously called external existence. The conception of reality becomes meaningless, unless an integral part, or aspect, is realized through at least one individual. What then is the significance of enlightenment on the part of an individual?

Here is conspicuously shown the significance of Buddha's attainment and revelation, by which he plays an integral part in the world's truth-order, and herein lies the importance of his personality as the Truth-winner and Truth-revealer. It is in his person that the real import of existence has come to light; it is in his enlightenment in the fundamental nature (*dhammatā*) of the world that the cosmos has found its own mouth-piece, the representative, the embodiment, of its truth-order; it is through his revelation that the world, including ourselves and many other beings of different sorts, has gained the key to the interpretation and comprehension of its real meaning. Knowing and seeing, enlightenment and revelation — all are nothing but the essential nature of the truth-order, by which the meaning of existence, and therefore of reality, is made explicit, or can be evolved. Wherefore it is said:

> The Exalted One knows knowing, sees seeing; he is the One who has become the eyes (of the world); he is the One who has become knowledge (or enlightenment); he is the One who has become truth; he is the One who has become Brahmā (the highest deity of Brahmanism); he is the instructor, the revealer, the One who pours out good, the One who gives immortality; the Lord of Dhammā, that is the Tathāgata. (*Samyutta*, 35. 116, etc.)

Buddha, the Tathāgata, is the prototypical representative of the seer, of the knower, of the one who has realized his own true nature, together with that of the whole world. In short, Buddha's enlightenment is the interpretation of the world, which means not simply a process in an individual mind, but plays an integral part in the existence of the world, being a revelation of its own meaning — a self-realization of the world, so to speak. This is the view of the Middle Path.

Now, let me further expound the Buddhist conception of the relation between the world and the individual, which gives the key to the understanding of its conception of reality.

The individual, as such, is neither real, in the commonly asserted sense of being a personally persistent entity, nor unreal, in the sense that it has no place in existence. It is unreal, because it is subject to constant change; but it is real, as a product of causation, as a manifestation of character accumulated by karma. Either of these points of view leads to the thesis, "There is no (substantial) *ego*." But Buddhism sees in the person of the Tathāgata a real individual, *the* individual *par excellence*, because the Dhammatā of the universe is represented, embodied, realized, in his person as the Tathāgata. It is in the personal enlightenment of universal truths in Buddha that the realm of Dhammā has come to self-consciousness, to the full realization of its meaning. In other words, the person of the Tathāgata is not an individual personality, in contradistinction to other individuals, but in communion with all others. When I say " all others," I mean it, not as an aggregate of separate individuals, nor as a haphazard crowd of individuals, but as unified in the basic unity of the Dhammatā, and united in the realization of the universal communion. This is the teaching of the *Ekayāna*, of which we shall see more presently. An individual, according to Buddhism, is no more a mere individual, if, and so far as, he identifies himself with others; his *ego* is transformed to a universal self. Buddhism does not call this transformed and expanded self a self, but a *Tathāgata*, or a " being of truth " (*dhammā-bhūto, dhammā-kāya*), as in the case of Buddha.

Looked at in this way, any individual is a Tathāgata who realizes the universal Dhammatā of the universe, not only in his ideas, but in his life, and lives the life of the universal self. So long as, and so far as, he regards himself as separate from others, every individual is only a partial, and therefore imperfect, manifestation of his own real nature (*dhammatā*), while every one is destined to attain the height, or depth, of his own true self in communion with all others, by virtue of the basic unity of the fundamental Dhammatā. When this ideal is attained, even partially, one has so far realized his real self, which is no longer an *ego* in the sense that he once cherished. He is the same person in appearance, but in reality his self is so far transformed. What thus happens resembles the metamorphosis of an insect. Buddha, in recalling his former lives, designates his former self by the pronoun " *I*," but he is at the same time most emphatic in distinguishing his former "*I*" — even the "*I*" when he lived as a prince or a recluse — and calls himself " Tathāgata," in the third person, as the designation of his true personality and high dignity. The same title may be applied to anybody who reaches the same attainment as Buddha; and, in fact, Buddha called every one of the same attainment a Tathāgata. In short, every one who has found his own real nature in the fundamental Dhammatā of all existences, that is, in communion with the Tathāgatas, is one who has become truth, become insight, and thereby identified himself with the universe. It is in the conception of reality attained by such a person that the universe is realizing its universal Dhammatā.

A necessary consequence of this idea about the relation between the individual and the world is the teaching of the Ekayāna. It means the one and the same way for all the Tathāgatas of the past, present, and future. It is the Way, and at the same time the Ideal — the way to realize the truth of universal communion, and the ideal to be reached by that way. It is also the foundation of existences, and the goal of the way, because an ideal is vain without foundation, and the two are simply two aspects of the same Dhammatā. Buddha said:

The Perfectly Enlightened of the past, and the Buddhas of the future,
As well as the present Perfectly Enlightened One who dispels sorrows from many —
All have lived, do live, or will live,
By revering Dhammā; this is the Dhammatā of all Buddhas.
(*Samyutta*, 6. 1. 2; com. *S.* 47. 18.)

This unity of the Ekayāna is manifested in the Buddhist community, which, though limited in its visible manifestation, is to be extended without limit to include all beings of every possible description, and of all ages. Thus, the Buddhist community is a realization of the universal communion of all Buddhas and Buddhas-to-be, who are—or ought to be—united in the revelation of the final Dhammatā. This is the reason why Buddha disdained any one who, being satisfied with the tranquillity of his mind, remains a solitary sage. Such a sage is called a Pacceka-buddha, or self-satisfied wise man, and is regarded not only as a selfish man, but one who does not see the real light, either his own, or that of the world. The Tathāgata, on the contrary, is an individual who is no longer an individual merely, but has identified himself with all others.

Thus, the Tathāgata is the ideal person in the Buddhist religion, and it is only in the life of the Tathāgata that the full meaning of the universe is realized. This ideal is called also Dhammā, which here means " norm," as Mrs. Rhys Davids correctly renders it. The moral norm and religious ideal for every Buddhist consists in attaining, as Buddha has shown by his own example, the supreme enlightenment in the truth-order and the fundamental nature of the world, in accordance with the truth of existence, and by treading the same One Road, in company with the Buddhas of all ages. The Buddhist ideal, seen in this light, necessarily demands the life of fellowship, in which the real continuity of life, or the Dhammatā of existence, is first realized. In this fellowship, an individual no longer remains a separate being, but becomes a personal embodiment of the universal life — " das Objectwerden des Subjects," to borrow the Hegelian terminology. The " communion of saints " transforms *our* self into the universal self; and therein is brought to light the true nature of reality.

To sum up, the Buddhist conception of reality is the existence in which the universal nature of existence is realized in the enlightened mind which is the realization of the all-embracing fellowship. It rejects reality apart from this personal enlightenment; it rejects an enlightenment in a secluded self — the former being externalism and the latter transcendentalism. But both aspects of being embraced and " aufgehoben " in the realization of the universal Dhammatā. In short, the true conception of reality is brought to light only in the unity of Buddha, Dhammā, and Sangha.

II. Tendai's Doctrines of the Middle Path and Reality

Tendai-Buddhism is a school representing, most faithfully and elaborately, the Middle Path of the Buddhist doctrine. It is a school founded, in the sixth century, by a Chinese monk from Tendai, named Chi-ki; and its chief aim was to achieve a higher synthesis of the external-realism of materialistic tendency and the acosmism of transcendental extreme. It further elaborated the theory of reality along the line of the thought above indicated, and on the basis of the "Lotus of Truth." This book, as has been observed above, may be called the Johannine Gospel of Buddhism. It tries to solve the problems of reality by the key given in the identification of Buddha's enlightenment with cosmic truth.

Omitting further reference to the book, I here cite a saying which became the starting point of Tendai's theory of reality. The saying is a verse in Nāgārjuna's *Madhyāmika Śāstra*, or Treatise on the Middle Path. It says:

> Everything arises according to causation;
> We regard it as a vacuity (*śūnyatā*),
> (But) it is phenomenal reality by virtue of appearance,
> Which is at the same time the Middle Path. (p. 503.)

Vacuity (*śūnyatā*, or *suññatā* in Pali) is an ancient term used in Buddhism, and meant something beyond common sense or ordinary ratiocination (cp., for instance, *Samyutta*, 55, 52; 20, 7; etc.). It was not a mere negation, as it is often understood; but speculations at which we must now glance clustered about it.

"Vacuity" was understood by the transcendentalists to mean the voidness of phenomenal things, and so the real entity was interpreted as being beyond all distinctions and causal relations. This position is most fully stated in the one hundred thousand *ślokas* of the Prajñā-pāramitā, a book aiming at "the annihilation of all relativities" by an almost endless repetition of ***neither, nor.*** But this annihilation was always carefully distinguished from the nihilistic view (*uccheda*) that nothing exists, because the Buddhist vacuity supposes a something beyond relativities, unknowable, yet attainable in meditation.[1] Now Nāgārjuna accepted the transcendentalist standpoint, but at the same time admitted an apparent reality (*prajñāpti*) in what is given (*upadā*). What he called the Middle Path was a synthesis of the two points of view. In spite of his adherence to the Middle Path, which was the precious inheritance of Buddhist thought, he did not give a definite statement of it, but left it to the domain of contemplative vision, attainable by only a select few. Thus, it was Tendai's task to draw a more positive and definite conclusion from Nāgārjuna's statement of the Middle Path, and for this purpose he translated the two extreme views into the terms of universality and particularity.

Vacuity, according to Tendai, means nothing but the non-being of a particular existence apart from the universal Dhammatā. We speak of this or that thing or substance, quality or condition, and think it to be a reality, in and by itself. Nothing is more erroneous than this, because we know that nothing in this world, visible or tangible, exists without causal nexus. It is a Dhammā, a thing or condition, because it is a manifestation of the Dhammā, the law of causation. Vacuity does not mean the voidness of any existence in itself, but vanity of the view that sees in it a reality apart from the fundamental Dhammatā.

Thus, the thesis of vacuity implies the antithesis, that what is apparently existing is a reality, in the sense that it is given, given as something the meaning of which must be sought deeper and higher. In other words, an abstract universality is a vacuity, not less than a mere particularity; either is a mere abstraction apart from a datum. A particular datum may be an appearance, and yet be a product of the universal law of causality, and a manifestation of the fundamental nature of existence. A thing or a con-

[1] It was this aspect of Buddhism, concisely put in the "Diamond Cutter," that attracted Lafcadio Hearn's poetic genius, and was connected by him with Spencerian agnosticism.

dition exists actually, and although it is subject to decay, and may disappear according to causality, it is so far a reality — a phenomenal appearance.

The synthesis amounts to affirming both vacuity and appearance at the same time. The conception of vacuity has shown us that a particular existence is void, when taken in itself; but it points to the reality of the universal, as an outcome of a thoroughgoing negation of relativity. On the other hand, the idea of phenomenal appearance has demonstrated that there is a reality in phenomena which is no less essential to our conception of being than the reality attached to the universal. The world of the universal, the unity of all things in the fundamental nature (*dhammatā*), is the foundation of every particular existence, pre-existent to all particular manifestations. Yet its manifestations in concrete beings, Dhammās, are as real as the pre-existent universals, being subject to the laws, Dhammās, which rule all. That they are ruled by the same laws shows their unity in the basis. The particular derives its being from the universal nature of things, while the universal could not fully realize its true nature without manifesting itself in a particular. Both are real, but either by itself is imperfectly real. The Middle Path consists in uniting the two aspects of existence, universal and particular, and in seeing therein the true reality. To this argument, the consideration of Buddha's personality gave the key, and we shall see how it is developed.

As to the relation between the particular and the universal, the case of Buddha is not only an example, but the typical representative. He was born as a human being, passed through mental struggles, and finally attained Buddhahood, and lived the fifty years of his ministry as the Truth-revealer. This is an actual life of a particular person, and no one can deny its facts, except the docetists,[1] against whom the orthodox Buddhists took a united stand. Yet he was a Buddha, because he was enlightened in cosmic truths and realized the universal nature of Buddha-

[1] Cp. the author's article on "Docetism (Buddhist)" in the *Encyclopaedia of Religion and Ethics*.

hood, which is called Bodhi, or Enlightenment. He is Bodhi incarnate, so to speak, and Bodhi is the universal and fundamental nature (*dhammatā*) of the spiritual existence, which is pre-existent to appearance of particular Buddhas, and the *a priori* basis of their attainment. The epithet " Tathāgata " is an adequate expression of the relation between the universal Bodhi and particular Buddhas. Buddha's personal life is a particular phenomenon, and the significance of his Buddhahood is lost, is a vacuity, when considered apart from the Truth he has attained and revealed to us. Yet the Truth (*tathā*) is a mere abstraction, a dead name, unless there appears a Tathāgata in concrete human life. The true reality in the person of Buddha consists in the dignity of the Tathāgata attained by a particular person, in virtue of the universal Bodhi which is the essential condition of his communion with the Buddhas of the past and of the future.

This solution of the relation between the particular and the universal in the person of Buddha as the Tathāgata serves, at the same time, as the solution of the questions which arose concerning the acquisition or inherence of Buddhahood. Buddhahood is an acquisition, viewed from the standpoint of phenomenal appearance, as is actually shown in the career of Buddha. But it is, at the same time, inherent in his nature, and also in each of us, because without the pre-existent universal Buddhahood, a Buddha loses the foundation of his dignity. He has become a Tathāgata by treading the same way, the One Road, as all other Tathāgatas, and by thus entering the communion of Buddhahood; and this apparent acquisition is the necessary development of the Buddhahood inherent in an individual and pre-existent to individual persons. The standpoint of the Middle Path thus emphasizes equally both the *a posteriori* acquisition and the *a priori* inherence of Buddhahood, because either one of these two aspects, without the other, is an imperfect idea of the Buddha as such. In other words, Buddha is really a man, and verily the Truth. As a man he has realized the truth of the oneness of existence; he is the Truth-winner. The person in whom the Dhammatā of the universe has come to light, and who has "become Truth," "become knowledge," cannot but be the adequate representative of the Dhammatā, that is, the Tathatā. The Lord of Truth, the Ruler of the Realm of Truth, derives his dignity from the very source of Truth, and therefore he can work as the Truth-revealer. The actual human manifestation is a condescension on the part of the universal Truth; while the latter is first embodied and actualized in the former.

The universal Buddhahood is called Dharma-kāya, or "Truth-body," while the personal Buddha is Nirmāna-kāya, or "Condescension-body"; and these two, together with another, the Sambhōga-kāya, or "Bliss-body," the spiritual manifestation of Buddhahood, make up the Buddhological Trinity. This doctrine of the Trinity is a very old one in Buddhism, and Tendai emphasizes the unity of the three, because the three aspects, considered as a unity, constitute the only right view of Buddha's person, and of the true reality exemplified *in* his person.

The Trinity of Buddha's person, however, is not limited to him alone, but in each of us is inherent the corresponding Trinity, or, as we may conveniently express it, the unity of the universal foundation and the particular manifestation. A concrete human being is a reality, but his full meaning is based on humanity in general. There is *a* man, and he is *the* man who would embody in his person the essential nature of humanity, not in the abstract, but concretely. The universal "humanity" is the "Truth-body" of every human being, and his life under particular conditions is his "Condescension-body," while his own self-consciousness, and the influence that he means to exert upon his fellow-beings constitute his "Bliss-body." In short, the unity of the universal man and the particular man is the reality of man.

The same remark applies to every other kind of existence, and Tendai assumes, in accordance with Buddhist tradition, ten different realms of sentient beings. The nethermost one is the hell (*naraka*), or rather purgatory, where beings of extreme viciousness, deprived of the light of wisdom, are tormented by their own vices. The furious spirit (*asura*) is a manifestation of hatred and greed; the hungry ghost (*preta*) represents never-satisfied greed, combined with stupidity; the beast (*tīryak*) is the life of stupidity and blindness; the heavenly worlds (*deva*) are the abodes of those beings who are intoxicated with pleasure and careless of others. These five, together with mankind (*manusya*), are the six stages of transmigration. Above these, are two kinds of beings who are self-satisfied in their own attainment in meditation or learning, and make no further effort to realize the vitality of the universal communion, represented by the learned *Śrāvaka* and the self-contented *Pratyeka-buddha*, above referred to. The *Bodhisattva* is a being, who, having attained a certain height of spiritual illumination, is striving earnestly for the salvation of others. Above them all stands Buddha, in whom the universal communion and the fundamental nature of all beings are realized in idea and life, and who, by virtue of his wisdom and mercy, leads other beings to the same light. Thus, in every being in each of these classes there is manifested the relation of the universal and the particular, the concrete life of the universal Dhammatā; but it is in Buddha alone that the full light of universal truths and the all-embracing communion are realized.

Though Tendai thus distinguishes the ten kinds of existence, he emphasizes the interchangeability of their natures and the interdependence of their existence. Take, for instance, the case of Buddha. Although he is above all others, he has in no wise lost the character of the others, or he could not arouse in himself compassion for others. Even in him, the nature of the extremely vicious is still inherent, the only difference between his nature and that of others being that in him the inferior qualities are subdued, and not allowed to work. Similarly with all others, even in the beings in the hells, Buddhahood, and humanity, and other capacities are still extant, though latent. Viewed in this way, the ten realms of existence and their respective natures are interchangeable and communicable. This point is formulated as the theory of the " mutual participation " of all existences; and since *all* ten are present, whether actually or potentially, in each of the ten, the interrelations among them are hundredfold, that is, ten times ten.

To develop and explain the doctrine of the "mutual participation," Tendai formulated the conditions of existence in any realm in the ten categories of being. The classification is taken from the Lotus, in which these categories are adored as the key to Buddha's insight into the world.[1] They are: 1. Essence; 2. attribute; 3. manifestation or mark; 4. potency; 5. function; 6. first cause; 7. secondary cause; 8. effect; 9. retribution; and 10. the consummate unity of all nine. We can easily see that these categories are nothing but an extension and amplification of the original tenet of causality (*paticca-samuppāda*).

By causality we usually understand today the necessary connection existing between an antecedent and its consequent. But the Buddhist conception of causality is more flexible, and is applied to the same kind of necessary link, to any relation of interaction, interdependence, correlation, or co-ordination, founded on an intrinsic necessity. The necessity may be a link existing between the beings or phenomena, or between the thing and the knowledge of it, or *vice versa*. In this respect, the Buddhist idea of causation covers the same ground as the *ratio efficiens*, as formulated in Scholastic philosophy. Although all these relations may finally be reduced to the terms of antecedent and consequent, the Buddhist would not confine the *causal* relation within the idea of *time* relation.

This is a consequence of the conception that all existences are correlated by the virtue of the same *dhammatā*, and that therefore the relations existing among them are mutual, both in reality and in thought. The cause, in the usual sense of the word, conditions the consequence, but the consequence no less condi-

[1] The formula is found in the second chapter of the book (p. 30 in the Kern-Nanjio edition). The Sanskrit text has five categories and their ultimate union: What (*ye te dharmāh*), how (*yathā te dharmāh*), of what condition (*yādṛsas te dharmāh*), with what marks (*yal-lakṣṇanās te dharmāh*), of what entity (*yat-svabhavās te dharmāh*), and the summation of the five.

tions the cause, though the mode of conditioning differs. A cause without its consequence is nonsense, and, at least so far, the former is conditioned by the latter. In this way, the application of causality was extended, and the formula of causality, cited above in the original wording by Buddha, may be applied to the ten categories, as the mutual relations conditioning one the other. Take, for instance, the categories of "essence," "attribute," and "mark." Because there is an essence, its attributes manifest themselves; because there are attributes, we know that there is the essence; because there are attributes, the marks appear; because there are marks, the attributes are discernible, etc. In this way the mutual dependence of the categories is established, and applied to the existence of every being, which is made up of a certain configuration and concatenation of the conditions, and in which the conditions of the categories are necessarily present.

It may make the position of Tendai clearer to speak, in this connection, of a division of Buddhist thought about the idea of causality. The question was whether causality should be understood as a serial causation or as a relation of mutual dependence, and the difference between the two conceptions involved the difference between a static and a dynamic view of the world.

The one school, which took the serial view of causality, traced, forward and backward, the evolution of the phenomenal world out of the primeval entity, and the involution of the former into the latter. The other school emphasized the interrelation and co-ordination of things, almost without regard to the questions of origin and final destiny. The latter was Tendai's position, and is known by the name "Reality-View," in contradistinction to the "Origination-View" or "Emanation Theory," of the other. Whatever the difference may signify, and whatever the original teaching of Buddha may have been, the "Origination-View" always inclined to take the derivative phenomena more or less as illusions; while the "Reality-View" devoted its attention to a close examination of existences as they are, and inclined to justify every being as a necessary phenomenon in the world of mutual interdependence. The former aims at reabsorption of the individual minds into the primeval Mind, while the latter sees in the full presentation of facts and relations the consummate realization of universal enlightenment. Thus, almost contrary to our expectation, the philosophy of the "Origination-View" is static, while the "Reality-View" tends to be dynamic. The theory of "mutual participation" was a result of Tendai's conception of causality in terms of correlation and co-ordination.

Another group of categories, to explain life in group (*dhātu*) is threefold: the *stage* on which a certain group of beings play their rôle and manifest their nature; the *constituents* which supply materials and components to the stage; and the *individuals* making up the realm.

Now all of these kinds of being, and the categories of existence, are essential to the consideration of reality, of the true nature of any being. The Middle Path view consists in taking up all these conditions of being, and in summing them up in one term, that is, "Reality" — the reality as it is, as it is conditioned, as it is grounded, and as it ought to be. Thus, in this view of reality is expressed the conception of Dhammā as the consummation of the various views held by different schools, and as the final unification of the manifold aspects implied in the term Dhammā. In fine, the Tendai Buddhist conception of reality consists in harmoniously uniting all aspects of existence, and in realizing the working of the many-sided Dhammā, even in one being; even in one particle of dust, as the followers of Tendai are fond of saying.

To recapitulate, Tendai had examined the manifold views of reality, and found justification in each of them; and his ambition was to unify them, by looking at every particular existence as if it were an adequate representative of the whole cosmos (*dharma-dhātu*). His conception of reality is equivalent to seeing everything *sub specie aeternitatis*, but his *aeternitas* differed greatly from that of Spinoza in being not monistic, but "according to the three thousand aspects" — ten realms to each of ten, this hundred in the ten categories of existence, and this thousand multiplied by the three categories of group existence.

CHRONOLOGICAL TABLE

The Period before Nichiren

A.D.	
500–800	The introduction of Buddhism and its establishment in Japan.
538 (or 552)	Buddhism officially introduced into Japan.
593–622	The reign of Prince-regent Shōtoku, the great organizer and patron of Buddhism.
720–760	The flourishing period of Nara, the era of " Heavenly Peace."
800–1000	The age of ecclesiastical organization.
767–822	Saichō, or Dengyō Daishi, the founder of the Hiei institutions, on the basis of Tendai Buddhism.
774–835	Kūkai, or Kōbō Daishi, the organizer of Shingon mysticism.
942–1007	Genshin, the abbot of Eshin-in, the greatest of the pioneers of Amita-Buddhism.
1000–1200	The age of ecclesiastical degeneration.
1157 and 1159	The civil wars which gave occasion to the rise of the military clans.
1159–1185	The reign of the Taira clan, in Miyako.
1186	The establishment of the Minamoto Dictatorship at Kamakura.
1200–1300	The age of religious reformation.
1133–1212	Hōnen, the propounder of Amita-Buddhism.
1155–1213	Jōkei, the reformer of Ritsu, or the disciplinary school of Buddhism.
1140–1215	Eisai, the introducer of Zen Buddhism, of the Rinzai school.
1200–1253	Dōgen, the great Zen master, of the Sōdō school.
1219	The Hōjōs thrust aside the Minamotos.
1221	The defeat of the Imperial party.

Nichiren's Lifetime

1222	Nichiren born (2d month, 16th day; March 30).
1233	Nichiren sent to Kiyozumi.
1237	Nichiren ordained; his religious struggles.
1243–53	Nichiren studying at Hiei and other centres of Buddhism.
1253	Nichiren proclaims his religion "to the universe" and to mankind (4th m. 28th d.; May 17).
1253–58	Nichiren on missionary journeys, and resident in Kamakura.
1258–59	Nichiren studying at the library of the Iwamoto monastery.
1260	"The Establishment of Righteousness and the Security of the Country" presented to the Hōjō government. (7th m. 16th d.; August 24).
1260	Nichiren attacked by a mob (8th m. 27th d.; October 3).
1261–63	Nichiren exiled to Izu (arrived there 5th m. 12th d.; June 11th).
1262	Nichiren formulates his five theses.
1263	Nichiren released and returned to Kamakura (2d m. 22d d.; April 1).
1264–68	Nichiren on missionary journeys, chiefly in his native province.
1264	The peril in the Pine Forest (11th m. 11th d.; December 1).
1268–69	Mongol envoys come to Japan.
1268	Nichiren renews his remonstrance and sends letters to the authorities and prelates (10th m. 11th d.; November 16).
1269–70	Nichiren on missionary journeys, probably in Kai.
1271	Nichiren returns to Kamakura, and the final issue fought.
1271	Nichiren arrested and sentenced to death; the narrow escape at Tatsu-no-kuchi (9th m. 12th d.; October 17).

1271–74	Nichiren exiled to Sado, an island in the Sea of Japan.
1271	Nichiren starts from Echi for Sado (10th m. 10th d.; November 13).
1271	Nichiren stays at Teradomari, the port for Sado, (21 — 27th d.; November 24–30).
1271	Nichiren arrives at Sado (28th d.; December 1).
1272	"Opening the Eyes" finished (2d m.; March).
1273	"The Spiritual Introspection of the Supreme Beings" finished (4th m. 25th d.; May 13).
1273	The graphic representation of the Supreme Being made (7th m. 8th d.; August 21).
1273	Several other important essays written.
1274	The sentence of release arrives at Sado (3d m. 8th d.; April 16).
1274	Nichiren arrives at Kamakura (3d m. 26th d.; May 4).
1274	Nichiren called to the government office (4th m. 8th d.; May 15).
1274	Nichiren leaves Kamakura (5th m. 12th d.; June 17).
1274–82	Nichiren lives in retirement in Minobu.
1274	Nichiren arrives at Minobu (5th m. 17th d.; June 22).
1274	"A Treatise on the Quintessence of the Lotus of Truth" finished (5th m. 24th d.; June 29).
1274	Mongols invade western islands, in autumn.
1275	"The Selection of the Time," and other writings.
1276	"In Recompense of Indebtedness," and other writings.
1277–78	The incident of Kingo, Nichiren's beloved disciple.
1281	"The Three Great Mysteries" finished (4th m. 8th d.; April 27).
1281	The great armada of the Mongols arrives at the Bay of Hakata (5th m. 21st d.; June 9).
1281	Nichiren sends a circular, the "Epistle of the Little Mongols" (6th m. 16th d.; July 3).
1281	The Mongol armada destroyed (int. 7th m. 1st d.; August 16).

1282	Nichiren leaves Minobu (9th m. 8th d.; October 10th).
1282	Nichiren arrives at Ikegami, and writes his last letter (9th m. 19th d.; October 21).
1282	Nichiren dies (10th m. 13th d.; November 14th).

The Period after Nichiren's Death

1300–1500	The rise of Nichirenite Buddhism and its conflicts with other forms of Buddhism.
1283	A convention of Nichiren's disciples; his writings brought together (the first anniversary of his death).
1289	The first schism; Nikkō deserts Minobu.
1294	Nichizō starts his propaganda in Miyako, later a great centre of the Nichirenite propaganda.
1295	Nichiji starts on a missionary journey to the north; believed to have gone to Yezo and Siberia.
1342	Nichizō, the great apostle of Nichiren, dies.
1314–92	Nichijū, the missionary in Miyako and in the north.
1385–1464	Nichiryū, the missionary in the central provinces.
1407–88	Nisshin, the persecuted.
1422–1500	Nicchō, the organizer of the Minobu institutions.
1536	The persecution of the era Temmon, the severest blow given to the Nichirenite movement.